FINAL SOLUTION TO THE RACE AND ECONOMIC PROBLEM IN THE USA AS SEEN BY GREAT WRITER FREDDIE L SIRMANS SR., A MUST READ.

AFRICAN AMERICAN EXCUSES, EXCUSES, EXCUSES, AND I'M SICK AND TIRED OF IT. WRITER ATTACKS BLACK LEADERSHIP.

Halt, stop, or brace yourself, because this great writer is fixing to let her rip, go on a tirade, rant, or what ever you may call it. OK, lets just dispense with any bull s... and just talk plain turkey. Sure, there is a lot of racism in America, always has been and always will be. Hell, I may be called a racist, but I think not.

Life is not perfect and this nation is not perfect, but it is the greatest country to ever exist in my view. I love this great country and it is the only home that I have ever known. This great country offers the most individual freedom and opportunity to ever exist on earth, and it still does in spite of our beloved tax and spends liberals, but still I love-um like a brother.

Now, as to my beloved African American race, the problem with us is too much pampering, period. Hell, I'm a neurotic mentally handicapped cripple from my childhood bed wetting days, yet I will never stoop to be just a plain excuse maker. If one accepts excuses for failure an excuse can always be found.

Sure, there may be a good reason for an excuse, but as for my self I don't want to hear it, I only accept results. Like a coach once said: "you show me a good loser, and I'll show you a loser." I have been counted

1

out all of my life. For me, I have always taken responsibility for my own survival and I know beyond a shadow of doubt that otherwise I wouldn't be standing today.

Today all I hear from African American leadership is what we lack, what we don't have, we don't have jobs, and on and on. However, the question that needs to be asked is: What do we need to do for our community our selves? Duh! And they will all look at each other like helpless sheep. Number one should be how could we provide more of our own jobs in our communities.

We African Americans have our racial priorities mixed up or maybe even misplaced in my view. Everyone's priority should be immediately family first, then community, city, state, country, but ones race can never be totally ignored to fit somewhere in that order.

One must have a mental identity to know who he/she really is as a person; otherwise one could end up with no true racial identity. Something of the sort has happened to the African American race on a mass scale.

We African Americans as a race mentally see ourselves as dependent like siblings that can't do for ourselves and must be taken care of by the master. And like most siblings we are jealous and compete against each other for the master's favors. That is why you see the herd mentality and we always vote anywhere from 90 percent to 99 percent for one party in almost every election.

We as a race are locked into this dependent sibling psyche. It is not a bad thing, it kept the African American race alive in an almost totally hostile environment right out of slavery. However, circumstance and the nation has evolved and that type of psyche is no longer needed for the black race to survive. Yet, the welfare state won't let blacks escape its dependent mentality.

The only thing that can break this dependency chain is for African Americans to be forced to stand on its own two feet. Folks, I don't have anything to do with reality, I am only telling things as I see them, you have the freedom to totally disagree with anything I write and brand me a fool and idiot, so be it.

The African American race in America is awesome; we hold many of the most powerful elected offices in this great nation, from the office of president on down. There is no logical reason why African Americans can't employ at least a quarter of the jobs in its own communities, yet I doubt its over 3 percent.

For God sake, grow up African Americans, grab the bull by the horns, and learn to love all people and especially those that look like you. Now, don't you go telling me you don't have hate and contempt for those that look like you? Otherwise, why else would there be all of these mass killings in black communities?

Plus, where you spend your money proves where your first loyalty priority lies and it's certainly not with the man in the mirror. No one is expected to support a dirty greasy spoon eatery, but remember Auburn Avenue and the likes in other cities could equal the best before the welfare state came about. Now, our elites run as far as affordable away from an all black neighborhood and it is all because of our welfare state.

The welfare state has reduced the once proud Negro race to a bunch of government dependent siblings that are constantly at each other's throat. We don't trust each other or truly respect each other and is ashamed of an all black neighborhood. And don't give me this bull excuse about high crime, the movie "Raising in the sun" proves blacks couldn't wait to get out long before crime was a problem.

If you don't love who you really are how can you expect other races to respect you. Liberalism is responsible for this sad condition and to this day still patronizes African Americans and hates nothing more than a black that's wants to be self sufficient and independent. A black conservative threatens liberal's ability to keep African Americans dependent minded and self-rejecting more than anything else.

You black man, you don't truly love your own people, you mentally see yourself like your master and better than that sassy nigger that is undeserving of respect. Besides, you see that sassy nigger as a competitor against you, why should you kiss his ass and help him to get ahead, f... him, I'll spend my money where I want too, and anyone that's got a problem with that can kiss my black ass. This is the type of thinking that goes on in the minds of so many in the African American community.

The only thing that can break this locked-in African American dependency mentality is to kick the young eagle out of the welfare state nest, then it will be forced to fly on its own, that is what the mother eagle does. What I just said is not cold and uncaring, that is being prepared to survive on ones own, and not disappear off this earth when this welfare state soon crashes.

The African American sad condition is the tip of the USA survival spear, or the canary in our culture mine. God save my beloved homeland. Hallelujah.

OK, OK, having aired it out and said my peace, what is the real solution to the African American problem? Anyone familiar with my work should know my constant drum beat for the only thing that can save all of America and even western civilization.

It is the economy, fool! Nothing on earth is more powerful than a genuine true free market place economy; it trumps the law and everything in terms of having and maintaining an orderly society.

However, the USA liberal socialist destroyed our true free market place economy almost eighty years ago by enacting the evil 1938 socialist minimum wage law. And the inner fabric of moral decay and culture rot along with a lack of any emergency bartering capacity has grown unabated ever since.

A true free market place economy must be absolutely free to have the power to discipline itself and the nation, the same as Mother Nature, with its supreme law of natural selection. There must be a survival need for anything in nature to exist, otherwise it starts ceasing to exist based on nature's supreme law of "Natural selection."

The enacting of the 1938 minimum wage law gave the USA government for the first time absolute power over private property rights and business production and distribution. That act for the first time allowed liberals to seize almost absolute power by operating a candy store and promising the moon and back.

Before the 1938 minimum wage law it was almost impossible to inflate the USA currency because the economy had the discipline power to purge out inflation, waste, inefficiency and the likes. Now, the minimum wage law acts, as a purge inhibitor and every imaginable negative anti-survival special interest group in America have grown like wild flowers unabated ever since. Mass killings in the womb and same sex marriages are just new additions to the anti-survival paths the USA is going down.

Negative anti-survival special interest is now a swamp with the coalition power to take down this great nation. Creating our minimum wage law purge inhibitor is like trying to stop nature's life and death cycle, insane. The evil 1938 socialist minimum wage law has an almost over-powering appeal to the economically ignorant, and has all but destroyed our culture, good morals, and any capacity to barter.

A nation can't have emergency bartering capacity without enough small farmers and home gardeners, which is what got the USA through the great depression. I could go on and on with the destruction this evil 1938 socialist minimum wage law has done to this great nation.

But, I will wrap it up by saying this: Everybody and his brother has an opinion, but it is my God given destiny to let you know until the 1938 minimum wage law is repealed it is impossible for the USA to be saved. The "Final solution" is to repeal this evil law, or we perish, period.

I believe all to no avail the federal reserve and politicians trying to save this welfare state beast will eventually sell the nations sovereignty, land, wealth, and mineral rights off like a hooker on the block. Plus, there is no telling what has already been sold off being $18,000,000,000,000 in debt already.

Only a handful of people know, but I seriously doubt there is any gold left at Fort Knox anymore. I can't make anybody believe me; still I believe I understand the workings of an economy as well as anyone. And I promise you this weak phony P.... of an economy the USA have today is almost as useless as tits on a boar hog in terms of saving itself or this great nation.

Repeal the 1938 minimum wage law and give the USA economy back its original power, please Sir/Madam. It is not about how much increase in wages that really count, it is about having a job to buy enough food and necessities to survive at all. What good is a higher wage if you can't afford hardy anything, duh? It won't happen overnight, but repealing the minimum wage law will wean inflation out of our currency so $1.00 will buy what $20.00 will today.

Folks, I don't have to be right on my assessment, and I even hope I'm proven wrong. Why oh Lord, why have

I been blessed with so much raw wisdom, it is like a curse, I see things so clearly, why me o-lord. Writer answers that himself: Why not you. Amen.
SIRMANS LOG: 07 MAY 2015, 1328 HOURS.

BALTIMORE SUPER MOM: I HAVE A DIFFERENT VIEWPOINT ON THAT MATTER. WHAT DO YOU THINK?
In fact this writer is out of phase with almost everything that goes on now a days. I take no joy in raining on anyone's parade or stealing anyone's thunder. I'm referring to the mom being praised for slapping her young son around and the news media even talking about making her woman of the year.

First let me explain my views on raising a well-balanced disciplined child. I believe corporal punishment is a supreme act of love in terms of long-term survival. Nothing instills a stronger conscious in a child than corporal punishment. A child raised with a balanced of love and discipline have by far the best chance of long-term survival.

I believe, used, as a last resort corporal punishment is a far more powerful form of love when raising the young. Many times the young will hate the one that gives them hard tough discipline. Today far too many parents see a child as a love item to be doted on, which I think is a terrible way to raise a child.

A child is a separate individual that should be taught responsibility and accountability to be a productive citizen many years later. Instead today many parents try to always please the child to make the child love them, which I think is a self-centered irresponsible parent.

The child that hated the disciplinarian most of the time years later will thank God for the only one who gave him the tools to survive. You see this intense almost spiritual like love many youngster years later will have for a hard nose strict disciplinarian sports coach. Now, back to the Mom that was slapping her kid around, God bless her.

I may disagree with her method but God bless her heart for caring and doing the best that she knew how to protect her child. I'm one that thinks a parent should never use their hands to discipline a child and especially a teenager. With parents of old that would be a complete no, no.

I believe when using corporal punishment and as a last resort one, two, three, or what amounts of licks should always be announced first. There is an old axiom that says: "A general should never give an order he knows will not be obeyed." And by the same token I don't think a parent should ever give a child corporal punishment unless he/she knows it will administer a fair amount of pain.

Otherwise, corporal punishment without pain just breeds contempt and disrespect. Just like when a mother tells a kid fifty times "Don't do that," to me in a reverse way that is actually teaching disobedience. The most important thing in child raising is consistence then the child will know what to expect.

But, when a child is allowed to disobey fifty times and on the fifty first time the parent is in a bad mood or fed up and backhand's the kid off a chair, that's no way to raise a child. Back to the kid being slapped around, he knew not to dare resist his mom, but he also knew he would not have to take any physical pain, too.

The truth of the matter is her type of behavior actually showed her lack of control over her son. A parent in complete control would have just said, go home I will deal with you later. And later at home she would have put two or three hard painful licks on his ass that would have really hurt.

I'm just glad I raised my kids over forty years ago; otherwise today I would be in jail.
SIRMANS LOG: 02 MAY 2015, 1305 HOURS.

IT'S A PHONY USA ECONOMY FOOL. WRITER LETS IT ALL HANG OUT IN DEEP, DEEP ANGER.
It is getting to where I am writing more and more notes or very short one or two paragraph articles. The reason is I have mostly said it all that truly matters, and to say more is just mostly a waste of my time.

Very few want a taste of my bitter medicine. Seems my great wisdom will only be appreciated after a lot of unnecessary great pain and suffering takes place in this great country. A lot of people in the USA know we have lost our way.

They know the country is in serious trouble, and can't survive on its present course. We have a situation like the seven blind men examining an elephant. One thought the legs were tree trunks, and another thought the tail was a rope.

The USA economy and the whole inner moral and culture fabric of the country are coming apart at the seams. The conservatives bless their hearts, at least they are aware and can see the handwriting on the wall and want to stop the madness.

Whereas the liberals are too shallow to be aware of or even know the economy is in danger of totally collapsing from too much spending. The liberal are hell-bent on starving the military and social spending this great nation out of existence, period.

Sure, the conservatives are aware of the over spending danger and wants to do whatever it takes to save our country, but in my view they doesn't have the perspective to see the big picture and will wild goose chase down endless false paths.

However, this is where my great supernatural wisdom comes into play and sets me apart from all but a handful. "There is always more than one way to skin a cat." And there are countless ways of saving the USA. However, I believe I am one of a handful with the deep, deep perspective to actually see the moving parts to proper dissect the USA economy.

I have the ability to see that the evil 1938 socialist minimum wage law took the discipline out of the USA economy. That caused the USA economy to be a phony weak P.... of an economy ever since that day. That almost 80 years ago fatal mistake must first be corrected before it is even possible to think about saving the great USA.

The USA must have a strong disciplined economy first before it will ever be able to save our culture, morals, or the economy itself and in that same order. This is fact, I see it, and I know it, but how many in power even know this or will agree with me on this, none is the answer.

So be it, I can shout it on the mountaintop, but I can't make anyone hear me. I love my country, and I'm mad, and I'm angry, but I know I must calm myself and continue the emergency distress call for USA survival, that is my destiny.
SIRMANS LOG: 29 APRIL 2015, 2032

A 2016 PRESIDENTIAL ELECTION MIND BLOWING ANALYSIS
I, Freddie L Sirmans Sr. believe the 2016 presidential election may become so polarized that hoards of Christians, independents, conservatives, etc. like never before will turnout and vote. November 2016 may be the most important United States election since 1776 in my view. It will determine if the United States

survives as a free nation or survives at all, period.

I, great writer if I had any real sense I wouldn't touch this hot potato issue with a ten-foot pole, but knowing me I have no business being a writer in the first place. The Dem's and liberals knows they must win the 2016 presidential election at all cost, or the evil 1938 socialist minimum wage law may finally be repealed. "I wish, the last part I just threw that in there for my sake, y'all."

Sure, there are a lot of republican candidates going for the 2016 presidential gold, but I believe the real drama and action is going to be on the Dem's side. The reason I say this is I think the real movers and shakers on the Democratic side doesn't think Mrs. Clinton can win this milestone election.

Of course, no one over there is ever going to admit to anything of the sort. But, "you can bet your bottom dollar that ways and actions always speak louder than words." Folks, I'm a writer and could be totally wrong on this whole matter, I'm just writing what I believe.

Still, I think the long political knives are being sharpened within the Democratic Party. And before this 2016 presidential election is over a lot of Democratic political blood is going to be spilled. In 2016 for the Dem's and the sake of their power everything is on the line, even the welfare state itself, and believe me the knock out drag out is not going to be pretty, y'all.

The smart money thinks the republicans will keep control of both houses of congress in 2016. That means if the republicans win the 2016 presidency they will have a trifecta, which means the liberal and Democratic Party power monopoly starting with the

"New deal" may finally be broken. Hallelujah. As you can see, all of the marbles are at stake for the liberals and Dem's. Myself, I see the dawning of a new day coming, people.

This is my one man's analysis of what's so much at stake here concerning this milestone 2016 election. We'll see, just how this real life soap opera ultimately plays out. Stay tuned.
SIRMANS LOG: 23 APRIL 2015, 1438 HOURS.

JUST A FEW WORDS OF WISDOM:
Economically wise, until our cruel evil 1938 socialist minimum wage law is repealed, no matter what the conservatives or the republicans do the game is still being played on a liberalism home court.

It is no longer a matter of if the great USA will be over powered by liberalism but how soon. If our phony hog-tied economy doesn't sink us first, we are already up to our neck in a vast moral decay and culture rotted liberalism swamp and the only relief in sight is repealing our evil 1938 socialist minimum wage law. But, I seem to be the only one with the God given wisdom to see the light on this, I pound and I pound, only to thick sculls and deaf ears.

So be it, I have filled my destiny and done my duty. I will start closing by saying this: Many people have endured great pain and suffering and said "They were actually glad it happened because it opened their eyes to things right before them that they could never see before." That is what has happen to the great USA, our liberal induced welfare state has lulled almost everyone asleep, the nation will just have to experience the pain and suffering and learn the hard way if the nation survives.

The prevailing thinking today is government owes us a living and is responsible for the people's survival. However, nothing could be further from the real truth, it is just the opposite. The people or private enterprise is responsible for the survival of government not the other way around; government is a parasite and can't survive unless the people support it.

The USA government is taking from 40 percent of the people and using that seized profit to take care of the other 60 percent of the people. Plus, we will soon be over 20,000,000,000,000 in debt and counting. Now, if anyone thinks this can last very much longer you are a dumb ignorant fool in my view.
SIRMANS LOG: 21 APRIL 2015, 0005 HOURS.

COLD REALITY CHECK:
Sure, anyone with an ounce of economic sense should know that the reasonable answer to the USA economy problem is to first balance the budget. But, the cold reality is the liberals have made so many voters government dependent that it is political suicide for any individual or political party to dare go there, and expect to remain in power.

It is just impossible to balance the USA budget without creating a smaller pie, which in the short run is going to cause some extra pain. And guess what, to hell with what's best down the road, what have you done for me lately is all that's going to matter in the voting booth for the masses of government dependents.

Race And Economic Problem Final Solution In USA

Obviously, politically no political party is ever going to be able to balance the budget to get control of the USA economy, period. However, no political party may be able to balance the budget but a true free market place economy definitely can.

Not only can a true free market place economy balance the budget, it will send liberalism packing and take our country back from all of these shallow minded do-good talking heads with weak survive instincts. The only true answer to saving the USA is not about getting lost on our phony hog-tied economy, immigration, or our insane foreign policy; it is about repealing the 1938 minimum wage law.

That will set free our hog-tied USA economy, then the economy will have the force and power to kick ass, send liberalism packing, balance the budget, and do what ever it take to save this great nation of individual freedom. Otherwise, there is not going to be a USA.

Take that as a dose of cold reality, writer, Freddie L Sirmans Sr. style. How do you like me now?
SIRMANS LOG: 10 APRIL 2015, 2228 HOURS.

Freddie L Sirmans Sr. weight losing helpful hint using the "Positive thinking" technique.
The definition of the positive thinking technique I'm talking about is: One takes a short saying or quote and repeats it over and over to ones self a minimum of fifty times or more every day.

It may take up to six months or more to start feeling strong results. This is the quote I use: "I can keep my body slim and healthy through God which strengthens me." Just leave God off or substitute another deity if one doesn't believe in God.

Lets face it folks, some of us like me are compulsive over eaters; I have suffered with this disorder ever since I was a child. Some of us just simply can't do it alone, that is why turning to God by saying through God, which strengthens me, is all-powerful.

However, it doesn't work over night, it takes a while to break through to the subconscious. But, if one stays the course long enough positive results will be realized.

Salt and sodium are the biggest factors in controlling high blood pressure. I buy the gallon jugs of drinking water with 0 sodium. Also, I buy the little squeeze bottles of fresh lemon juice and drink lemon water as my main beverage, no sugar added for me. I believe some water is loaded with sodium for the same reason as processed foods, be aware.

NOTE:
There is a simple universal fact about life and survival, risk and struggle is a greater part of it. If too much risk and struggle is taken out of life, then its purpose and value greatly diminishes. It is in our DNA from evolving over the eons. Repealing our evil 1938 socialist minimum wage law will rescue the USA from our dying liberal welfare state, which has made the USA a P.... of a society.

NOVEL: A SECOND CHANCE TO LIVE III, BY FREDDIE L SIRMANS SR.

17

CHAPTER 1

Rufus Thomas was relaxed and happy on this Friday afternoon as he was taking down the   steam table out front in the dining room, when all of a sudden he heard shots and glass breaking. Then it occurred to him like being awaken out of a dream that someone was shooting into the restaurant. Without a second of delay, he instinctively fell to the floor.

As he lay on the floor, his mind raced back to an incident that had happened in his parking lot about a week ago. Within the last two weeks, a group of young teenagers had started using his parking lot to make drug deals. Therefore, last week, he decided to put a stop to it.

He put his 9mm (9-millimeter semi-automatic handgun) in his pocket and walked out to the parking lot keeping his hand in his pocket on his gun. "Hey you kids, don't y'all know this is private property?" said Rufus in a strong firm voice. One of the kids, who looked to be around 15 or 16 replied, "We have a right to be here."

"Not on my property you don't. I'm telling you to get off my property right now before I call the cops."

"And if we don't?"

"That's your choice."

After swearing and grumbling, they slowly moved off down the street. After a couple of days, Rufus decided to put the incident out of his mind. A voice yelling, "Mr. Thomas, Mr. Thomas is you all right?" brought him back to the present and to his feet. It was Zaporia Monique one of the two servers that worked for him. "Mr. Thomas, what happen? Are you all right?"

"I think so, Zaporia. Someone was shooting through the windows. I believe those kids I ran off the property about a week ago had something to do with this." Erica, the other server who worked at the restaurant, had come out of the kitchen to see what all of the commotion was about. "Its okay, Erica Laverne you and Zaporia go ahead and finish cleaning up, and I'm going to call the police."

Bruce Allen was born in Buieville, GA. He learned early growing up in the Jimmy Carroll housing projects that you had to watch your back and fight to survive. Bruce loved his mother with all his heart but had only contempt for a father he had never met who deserted his mother before he was born.

His mother tried her best to make him go to school, but he had become more interested in making money. He had learned that money meant power, the ability to get pretty women, and the nice things in life. The youth gang in the Jimmy Carroll housing projects was called The Young Vipers. The Young Vipers' ages ranged from twelve to sixteen.

Bruce joined The Young Vipers as soon as he became eligible. By the time Bruce turned age fifteen, he was the undisputed leader of The Young Vipers. No one becomes a leader of the gang without being brutal, cunning, and savage. Some things Bruce Allen could forgive a person for, but disrespecting him was the unforgivable sin, and whoever crossed that boundary had to pay.

Growing up in the Jimmy Carroll housing projects, Bruce was no stranger to the drug business. As long as he could remember, the most successful people he knew were drug dealers. They had money, pretty women, and new cars. What else could one want? That was everything. At a very young age Bruce started in the drug business at the very bottom.

For a few dollars he would work as a lookout for the dealers and warn them if the cops were approaching. Now, he had graduated to doing a little dealing himself. Last Friday down on Mary Alice Ave., Bruce was about to close his biggest drug deal yet, when this old stooge had to come out and mess everything up. It is a perfect location for dealing drugs.

19

Race And Economic Problem Final Solution In USA

It is located off to the side where you can see who is approaching from a great distance. This is a free country, he thought. Who does that old stooge think he is going around at old disrespecting people? A few days after the incident, Bruce and a few of The Young Vipers were hanging out at Regina's Cafe. Still fuming about being disrespected, Bruce said to his second in command, "You know, Boom Boom, that parking lot down on Mary Alice Ave. is the best drug dealing location I know of.

"You're right Bruce," replied Boom Boom, "we could have that parking lot all to ourselves if nobody was in that building. I think if somebody stole a car, drove by, and shot up the place that would teach that old stooge a lesson."

"Boom Boom, I believe you're right," said Bruce.

At Buieville Police Department on Friday afternoon, Lieutenant Marvin Elder was anticipating a relaxed weekend with his family. Maybe we'll take the boat out on the lake for a few hours, he thought. Lt. Elder came from a long line of lawmen; his granddad was a deputy sheriff and two of his uncles were policemen. But his father didn't want any part of law enforcement. His father became a fire fighter.

After over eighteen years on the Buieville Police Department, Lt. Elder was nearing retirement. He started off as a foot patrolman in and around the Jimmy Carroll housing projects, which is one of the roughest neighborhoods in the city. Over the years, he served in the Traffic Division, Detective Division, Internal Affairs Division, and NARC. Division. Then about a year ago, they picked him to head up the new Youth Gang Division.

Lt. Elder was in the process of finishing up his daily reports, when his secretary Carolyn Laverne yelled, "Lt., pick up line two."

"This is Lt. Marvin Elder, may I help you?"

"Lt. Elder, this is Rufus Thomas. I operate The Harlem Garden Restaurant at 1401 S. Mary Alice Ave. We just had a drive by shooting down here."
"Was anybody hurt? "asked Lt. Elder.
"Fortunately not, I was the only one out front in the dining area; luckily my two waitresses were back in the kitchen. Also, I hit the deck after the first blast."
"Did you see the car that did the shooting?"
"Before I hit the deck I caught a glimpse of gray, but I couldn't tell what make or model it was." "
"Do you know how many shots were fired?"
"I can't be for sure. Maybe three or four shots, everything happened so fast I just can't be for sure."
"Mr. Thomas have you had any dissatisfied customers or disputes with anyone recently."
"Yes, as a matter of fact I believe I know who is behind this whole thing. It began about two weeks ago when some teenagers started what looked to me like drug dealing in my parking lot."
"Did you call the police?"
"Maybe I should have. But you know how it is, drugs are so bad. You know they are going to do them; you just hope they do them somewhere else. But last Friday afternoon I got fed up and went out there and told them to get off my property, or I would call the cops."
"Mr. Thomas, I need to warn you. You are definitely risking your life confronting these gangs. They are young, but don't let that fool you; these kids are gang members and they will not hesitate to hurt you. Mr. Thomas, it will take me about thirty minutes to get down there to investigate the scene and ask you a few more questions."
"Maybe I can track down this gang who has started using your parking lot. But Mr. Thomas, I suggest you take precaution, because this drive by shooting is probably the first attack in a war on you and your property."

21

Race And Economic Problem Final Solution In USA

While pulling into the parking lot at the Harlem Garden Restaurant, Lt. Elder's professional trained eye alertly surveyed the parking lot and surrounding area.

He quickly saw why someone dealing drugs would like this location. The parking lot was located on the side of the building with just enough shrubbery to conceal a small group of people. It was isolated enough to allow early warning when to co someone was approaching. The restaurant was not very large, it probably had a seating capacity of around fifty people. The building and landscape were clean and well kept.

Pushing through the front door, he quickly noticed the liberal use of wood grain and honey colored paneling. He sensed that he would be dealing with a very conservative individual. The color scheme was pine green, navy blue, with a few spots of burgundy. The place seemed almost regal. It definitely was no cheap greasy spoon.

He noticed a man behind the serving line. "Hello sir, I'm Lt. Elder from Buieville P.D..."

"Hello, Lt. I'm Rufus Thomas the owner of this restaurant."

Lt. Elder walked to the back wall opposite the two bullet shattered front windows. Reaching into his pocket he pulled out a small leathermen's tool, then he proceeded to dig out what looked like a 9mm slug.

He next found three other bullet holes. "Mr. Thomas, your estimation of the number of shots seems to be right," said Lt. Elder. "In all I counted four bullet holes. Mr. Thomas, I would like for you to tell me everything you can think of about the kids you ran off your property last week. Did you notice anything unusual or out of the ordinary? Did you notice any scars, any limps, speech impediment, or anything that may help to identify this gang?"

There are over fifty gangs in this city, it is almost like finding a needle in a hay stack. "I'm sorry Lt., they just seem like ordinary kids," said Mr. Thomas.

"Here is my card, Mr. Thomas, please give me a call if you think of anything later that might help me find this gang. Also, give me a call if you see anything that's out of the ordinary, like the same car going past your restaurant more than normal."

"I certainly will, thank you Lt," said Mr. Thomas.

CHAPTER 2

Marion Harris, aka Loco Harris, was one of four siblings from a middle class family. One of the many baby boomers born after WWII, his father was a postal worker and his mother was a school teacher. Young Marion was an A student because that is what his parents expected of him. After high school he enrolled in a top Ivy League school. His major was ancient history. Marion was raised in a Protestant family, but in college he was exposed to people of many different religions.

Being sort of a free spirit, Marion decided to study and experiment with different religions. Shortly after getting his undergraduate degree, Marion received a draft notice. Sure, he believed that he could have enrolled in graduate school and gotten a deferent, but he decided that he would fight for his country. A year or so later Marion was a member of The Big Red 1 fighting in the jungles of Nam (Vietnam).

During his tour in Nam, Marion manage to avoid physical injury to himself, but the stress of witnessing many of his buddies being blown to bits took a mental toll on him.

Traumatic flash backs soon started invading his dreams at night. Even after getting out of the Army and returning home, the flash backs could strike without notice. No one seems to know exactly how or when Marion acquired the nick name

"Loco Harris". It is said some guy on the streets started calling him that and it stuck.

Loco never married and now spends much of his time pushing a grocery store cart around town picking up aluminum cans. Loco does get a check from SSI, SSD, or somewhere.

His sister Drunell manages his money and makes sure he always has room and board. His sister Drunell won't give him much spending money because he will drink it up in beer or let the street women talk him out of it. That is why he goes around picking up aluminum cans to get beer money.

Make no mistake about it, Loco is still an intelligent man despite his mental condition. From time to time he will clean up and eat breakfast at the Harlem Garden Restaurant. If asked, Loco likes to give lectures on world religions that he acquired great knowledge on during his college days. Most week day mornings Rev. Whitehurst, Deacon Bines, Deacon Jones and a few other retirees eat breakfast and drink coffee at the Harlem Garden Restaurant. They all are senior citizens and retired.

They know that Loco had tried different religions as a young man in his college days. They liked to ask him what he was that day, a Buddhist, a Hindu, a Moslem, or some other religion. They also knew that would set him off on one of his lectures. They tend not to take him seriously and will chuckle and crack a few harmless jokes. But, never will they be mean or cruel, because they all love Loco.

Loco has told them that he believes in a superior being, and it doesn't matter if it is called God, Allah, Jehovah, or whatever name. He believes there has to be a focal point or control point somewhere or somehow. He believes that even our sense of logic, which we cannot escape, had to be preprogrammed into us by some unknown organized source in some space and time.

He stresses that modern science is discovering by means of supercolliders that space and time is not fixed, and that no one knows what space and time really means. Loco believes human beings are some type of super, super self regenerating computers that are programmed with logic. We all experience reality mainly through our five senses. Who really knows, we may have many more senses that we are not aware of. We are chemical and electrical beings. Everything about us operates on a chemical and electrical basis. Even our thoughts Loco believe are made up of electrical impulses, wave lengths, and frequencies that are far too advanced for modern science. Out of our five senses of sight, sound, taste, touch and smell, far more advances have been made in the first two.

Through means of modern cameras, transmitters, and receivers man can see and hear what is happening anywhere on earth and far into outer space.

Electronics have come a long way since the early days of large vacuum tubes, super heterodyne receivers, and crude cathode ray picture tubes. There is some progress in extending the sense of smell. There are a few crude devices around that can imitate the smell of a few items on a computer screen. At some point in our near future there will probably be a device that will imitate the smell, touch, and taste of anything we see on a TV screen.

Janet Thomas loved her work as a nurse at Betty Gertrude Memorial Hospital. Ever since she was a little girl she had wanted to help and care for people. On Fridays Janet loved to have dinner out or have some friends over. But it's been a while since she shared a quiet dinner at home alone with her husband Rufus.

Janet eased her brand new, willow green and burgundy colored vinyl top Towncar into traffic. She was accustomed to the thirty minute drive to their ranch style home on Debra Marie Drive in Woodgate Heights. As the town car begin to cruise, Janet thought back to when she was twenty-years old. Then Janet Brown, she attended Walter Bernard Community

College in San Diego. She remembered, through her best friend Minnie Martin, she was introduced to a young Navy Petty Officer named Rufus Thomas.

At first he seemed too serious for her taste, but slowly she realized it was a facade to cover up his real shyness. Underneath he had a genuine dry wit sense of humor. As Debra Marie Drive came into view, it brought Janet back to the present.

She checked her watch as she slowed the Towncar and turned right onto Debra Marie Dr. The time was five P.M. She was expecting her husband Rufus to arrive home around five thirty.

Leroy Jackson and Rufus Thomas had been friends ever since their high school days. Not a week went by that they didn't go fishing, bowling, play a game of chess, or do something together. Leroy's wife Patricia hated Rufus' political views. Leroy's political views tended to be moderate, but his wife Pat was a true bleeding heart liberal.

Pat was always telling him, "For the life of me, Leroy, I don't see why you like to hang around with that damn Rufus Thomas. I believe he is some kind of extremist rightwing nut or something. Always blaming everything on big government and the welfare state. How the hell does he think poor people and the homeless are going to survive without welfare and food stamps. I can't pay my bills as it is. I'm down to my last dollar. I sure hope they hurry up and call my number on the lottery."

Leroy enjoyed their friendship. Most of what Rufus said went in one ear and out the other. But Rufus was right about welfare and the social programs destroying the family and the extended family unit in this country.

Before pushing the key pad buttons to arm the security system and lock the front door, Rufus decided he best take Lt. Elder's advice on being cautious. He didn't always carry his handgun on him, but until this gang was caught, he planned on being prepared to defend himself at all times. He put his 9mm in his pocket and locked up.

As he merged his Silverado into traffic heading home, he thought every American should thank God they lived in a country with the freedom to bear arms, it is the rare exception, not the rule. Liberals are spouting the big lie when they say it would be safer with no guns. The real threat to our freedom and safety is not the criminal with a gun, he is only doing what he is allowed to do.

The real threat to our freedom and safety is the shallow minded liberals who allow creeping socialism to prevail. The main reason the founding fathers enacted the second amendment was not for hunting and personal protection, but as a last resort to save individual freedom from an all powerful government out of control. The fact is, there is no way we could have and continue to keep the freedoms we take for granted in this country without the freedom to possess arms. It was almost six p.m. when Rufus eased his Silverado into his carport.

After quietly letting himself in the carport door, he heard the pleasant voice of his wife saying, "Hello dear."

"Hello," said Rufus walking over to the counter near the sink where she was making a salad. Rufus gave his wife a quick kiss on the lips. "Janet," said Rufus, "a bad thing happened at the restaurant today. We had a driveby shooting."

"Oh my God! Why would anybody want to do that?", she moaned.

"I can't be a hundred percent sure, but I believe some kids I ran off the property about a week ago had something to do with it. I told Lt. Elder from the Buieville Police Dept. about the kids I ran off the property, and he seems to think they belong to one of the youth gangs operating in the city. Lt. Elder also believes the gang has declared war on me and my property."

"Rufus, you know I have asked you in the past to relocate your business out of that god forsaken area, you see how the surrounding neighborhoods have changed in the last few years."

"Gang or no gang, I am not going to let a group of kids run me off my property."

"But sweetheart, promise me you will at least consider relocating."

"Okay; I promise."

"Good, said Janet. "Now you go ahead and clean up; I'm preparing us a nice candle light dinner."

As the shower water sprayed over his body, Rufus let his mind drift back to when he was a young Navy Seaman stationed at San Diego. The Navy had trained him to be a cook, but on his off-duty time he decided to take English 101 at Walter Bernard Community College.

There he got to know a young lady in his English class named Minnie Martin. At a party, Minnie introduced him to Janet Brown. At first, he thought Janet was too much of the party type for him, but he soon realized she was one of the most selfless people he had ever known.

She loved her friends, but they would never take the place of a stable home life. They got engaged, and a year later they were married. The aroma of Janet's home cooking brought him back to the present. Once they sat down to the candle light dinner and the blessing was said, Rufus thought just how much he had to be thankful for.

He had a beautiful and charming wife, a lovely daughter, Freddy Mae, who had finished college and had a career of her own as a computer programmer, and most of all he still had his life, health, and strength. Hearing Janet say, "How do you like the food Rufus?" brought him out of his deep thoughts.

"Sweetheart, it tastes great, you know how I just love your down home cooking."

After the meal they moved to the sofa in the den. They sat side-by-side on the sofa with Janet leaning gently against his chest. As they listened to their favorite oldies, Rufus gently stroked and caressed Janet's neck and shoulder area. Every now and then he would kiss her gently. As time passed, the kisses became regular, then, more regular and passionate, still, more regular and passionate, releasing his embrace, he gently lead her to the bedroom. Later as they lay in each others arms totally spent, they told each other how much they loved each other. Relaxing in bed after making love, Rufus liked to express his political philosophy as long as Janet would stay awake.

Without a reply sometimes, he would talk for thirty minutes or more. "You know, Janet," said Rufus, "when I see young kids committing all of these crimes. Sure, you have to blame them primarily, but it goes much deeper. The real blame is the welfare state and the parents. All throughout history, the male carried out discipline in the home until within the last fifty years.

"Before fifty years ago this country never had a problem with family values or ill-raised youngsters. Then around fifty years ago, welfare and the social programs took over the role of ed to provider and daddy, without enforcing discipline. The first thing the welfare and social provider did was demand that no man could live with his family if they received government aid.

That order drove off the one that had maintained family values and discipline all throughout history.

"With welfare and social programs being the real provider, the on hand female became only a stand-in provider. Both of these new providers failed to carry out the first duty of being a provider. That primary duty was to maintain family discipline and values. With raising young men, some women can be tough and do a good job, but most can't or won't do the job.

Now, with the welfare and social program tentacles extending all throughout this society, true family discipline and family values in most cases are something from the past. That is the cause of our present state. Most of the kids in these gangs have never had any real discipline. These kids have never been conditioned to fear real punishment or consequences for improper behavior.

"The only way to bring back the strong family and extended family system is for the government to wean itself out of the role of uncle sugar daddy. It's only since the big government sugar daddy booted the man, for the most part, out of the provider role that so many of our young men are being lost to drugs and violence.

"All that is necessary for us to solve our social problems is for the government to get out of people's lives as much as possible. Sure, there will be hardship and suffering, but it has to be a natural selection process, otherwise any do-good human tinkering is only going to compound the problem and make it worse.

"Another thing, is all of this hollering about jobs going overseas. What's missing here is the jobs are being driven overseas by big government, high health cost, high taxes, environmental laws, and other big government mandates.

"It's a matter of survival, no business can compete and survive unless it makes a profit. There must be something an ordinary citizen can do to make a difference. Janet, you know, I think I'll try writing a book. Janet, said Rufus a little louder. zzzzz, zzzzz, zzzzz.

"Oh well, it was a good idea anyway," said Rufus as he turned over on his left side, his favorite sleeping position.

Tonight he was sure he would sleep like a baby.

Race And Economic Problem Final Solution In USA

Bruce Allen was age sixteen, and his mother Miss Gracie Bell Allen thought he was in school everyday. Sure, Bruce would leave home every school day morning; but instead of going to school he would spend the day playing basketball and at his girl friend's LaTonya's house. LaTonya was on welfare, but you wouldn't know it because she lived in a nice home in a nice neighborhood.

LaTonya had just turned eighteen years old and had two kids. Bruce's favorite hangout was Regina's Cafe. Miss Felicia Regina, the lady that owns the cafe, would sometimes get her niece LaTonya to come down and help her out at the cafe. A little over a year ago, Bruce started trying to talk to LaTonya, but she wouldn't have anything to do him because she felt he was too young for her.

A few months later, some guy started giving LaTonya a hard time. After a while Bruce walked up to the guy and said in a low but strong, firm tone of voice, "Listen buddy, I'm going to ask you only one time to leave the lady alone." The guy just stared at Bruce for several seconds, then said, "So that's the way it is?"

"That's the way it is," replied Bruce. The guy said he didn't want any trouble and left.

About a week later, LaTonya invited Bruce over to her house. Now over a year later Bruce and LaTonya are still seeing each other. Bruce tells her he loves her and wants to buy her a car and some of the finer things in life. After spending most of the day with LaTonya, Bruce, Boom Boom, and a few other gang members were scheduled to meet that evening at Regina's Cafe for an important meeting.

Later that evening, Bruce told the gang members that he didn't want to kill the old stooge, he just wanted to drive him out of business and teach him a lesson. "Bruce, you must be getting a little soft. This guy is armed and dangerous," said Boom Boom.

Bruce thought that it may be only a matter of time before he would have to put Boom Boom in his place. "Okay," said Bruce, one last time, "Everyone is expected to have two cans of spray paint. We will arrive at the building in groups of three and leave in groups of three. The job shouldn't take over five minutes. The strike time is ten o'clock. Any questions? No questions? Then I'll see you guys tonight."

One advantage of being a long time cop is you have time to develop a lot of information sources. Monday morning Lt. Elder logged out to some of the roughest neighborhoods in the city. The first stop on his list was the Jimmy Carroll Housing Project.

Before leaving, he decided to give his secretary Carolyn Laverne some last minute instructions. "Carolyn, I want you to check with the record section and see if they have any reports of gray cars being stolen within the last week. If so, find out who found it and any information they have on it."

"Yes sir, I will take care of that right away."

"I'll be out of the office all morning, but I should be back around noon.

"I'll have my portable in case I have to be reached in an emergency."

"Yes sir." It had been quite awhile since Lt. Elder had visited the Jimmy Carroll Housing Project.

His mind raced back to about thirty years ago when he was a young man. He remembered growing up in the Little Miami section not very far from the Jimmy Carroll Housing Project. Back then the projects were a very decent and respectable place to live. As a senior in high school, he used to play sand-lot football and date girls in the projects.

They had a fine community center and basketball courts. But like a lot of housing projects around the country, it has degenerated because of crime and drugs. To keep from completely losing it to crime and drugs, the Buieville Police Dept. located a precinct station there and started foot patrols.

32

He was brought back to the present as the five story white brick buildings came into view.

Lt. Elder decided to park in front of the office but not because he had any intention of going inside. He was sure he still had a couple of long time contacts still around. Since it was about nine a.m., there was hardly anybody outside standing around. That suited him fine because a lot of people were suspicious of anyone talking to a cop for any reason.

Lt. Elder decided to try Littlejohn's apartment to see if he was home. After reaching Littlejohn's apartment, he pulled the screen door back and gave three loud, quick raps on the door.

After a few seconds, he thought he heard a slight movement inside. Then after waiting several more seconds, he again gave three loud, quick raps. This time he was sure he definitely heard someone approaching the door. Then a voice barely audible from the inside said, "Who is it?"

"Lt. Elder."

"Who?"

"Lt. Elder," he said much louder.

"Just a minute." After what seemed like a full minute, a very small man cracked the door about six inches. "What can I do for you Lt.?" As Lt. Elder looked at Littlejohn he wondered what motivation, or lack of motivation causes people to throw away their life. Littlejohn stayed away from crack and the hard drugs, but as Lt. Elder peered at his face and eyes he could see that cheap wine and rot gut liquor had certainly taken its toll.

"Littlejohn, I would like to come in and talk to you for a couple of minutes," he said.

Littlejohn opened the door wide and stood aside. Lt. Elder strode inside a few feet, then pivoted around to face Littlejohn.

"Littlejohn, I want to know what the word on the street is if any, about a driveby shooting on the Harlem Garden Restaurant last week." lips.

"The word is, it was one of the young gangs," said Littlejohn.

"Do you have any names?"

"No, that's all I've heard on it."

Lt. Elder reached into his pocket and pulled out a clip of bills and slid off a couple of twenties and told Littlejohn, "I want names."

"Give me a couple of days," said Littlejohn.

"Here is my card; give me a call the minute you get a name."

Leaving the Jimmy Carroll Housing Projects Lt. Elder then made a couple more contacts. The time was around noon so he decided to pick up some fried rice, sweet and sour pork, a couple of egg rolls and head on back to the office.

Rufus used to keep the Harlem Garden Restaurant open until 9 o'clock at night during the week and until 11 o'clock on Friday and Saturday nights. But about a year ago, he started closing around three thirty in the afternoon Monday through Thursday and nine p.m. on Friday and Saturdays because his older customers didn't like to come out at night due to crime.

Since the driveby shooting, Rufus made sure he was armed most of the time. He was constantly on the alert for any sign of trouble, but so far everything was quiet and normal around the Harlem Garden Restaurant. Rufus wanted to finish cleaning up and close on time this afternoon because Monday nights was his church league's bowling night.

Five members from their church made up their bowling team. The five members were Rufus Thomas, Leroy Jackson, Brenda Johnson, Danny Hebert, and Freddie Lee Jr. Rufus would usually pick up Leroy and they would meet the others at the bowling alley at 8 p.m. After Rufus finished watching the six o'clock news and

Crossfire, he decided to go pick up Leroy and head to the bowling alley.

Pulling up at Leroy's house Rufus got out and rang the door bell. Rufus thought people who pulled up to a person's home and sit there blowing the horn were displaying laziness and ill manners. Why distract or wake up the whole neighborhood?

Someone from inside the house said, "Who is it?"

"Rufus."

"I'm coming," said Leroy. By the time Rufus got back in the Silverado, Leroy was coming out the front door. "How is it going, Rufus? "said Leroy as he climbed in the passenger side of the Silverado.

"Doing pretty good; how about you?"

"I think I'll make it." Rufus backed the Silverado out and headed toward the bowling alley.

"Leroy," said Rufus, "do you think any one race is more intelligent than others?"

"I never thought much about it, but I don't think so," said Leroy.

"I don't think so either, but I do believe there might be a cultural factor that affects motivation.

" I believe motivation affects one's intelligence and achievement more than anything else in life, but it is almost always ignored. In every race there will be a smart high range and a dumb low range of intelligence. Everyone can learn to be more intelligent, some just have to study and work at it harder. This is when motivation is all important.

"The big question is, why are some people highly motivated and others not motivated at all? Some cultures seem to highly motivate its members, whereas other cultures don't seem to motivate its members at all. In many cases, the more normal and contented one is, the less motivated one is. As a rule, those searching for love and approval are the most motivated and highest achievers of all. In my view the most motivated of all are insecure individuals with a need to love or be loved."

35

"Rufus," said Leroy, "will you do me a favor? Ask me if I care, it's all nonsense." Rufus didn't reply as he turned the Silverado into the bowling alley parking lot.

Inside the bowling alley, Rufus and Leroy greeted the other players who were waiting on their arrival. Their team managed to beat the Harrington All-stars, one of the toughest teams in the league. After saying good-by to two of the younger players, me onl Danny Hebert and Freddie Lee Jr. Brenda Johnson, the nurse and only female member of the team, walked with him and Leroy back to his truck.

Saying good-by to Brenda, Rufus then dropped Leroy off and headed home to Janet. Once home and showered Rufus climbed into bed.

"Are you awake Janet?" said Rufus.

"Yes Rufus, I was just about to doze off, but I am fully awake now." They snuggled together in each others arms, gently kissing and anticipating, but not rushing to that distance, slowly approaching, then faster, still faster explosive ecstasy.

When Rufus arrived at the Harlem Garden Restaurant the following morning, he could hardly believe his eyes. Someone had scrawled racial graffiti all over his building. After he got inside Rufus immediately called Lt. Elder. He was told Lt. Elder didn't get in until 8 a.m., but he would get in touch as soon as he arrived.

Rufus was back in the kitchen preparing breakfast when the phone ring about eight fifteen. "Harlem Garden Restaurant," said Rufus.

"This is Lt. Elder, may I speak to Mr. Thomas?"

"This is he."

"I got a message you wanted me to get in touch with you?"

"Yes, I wanted to report that last night somebody scrawled racial graffiti all over my building."

"Mr. Thomas, most likely it was that same gang that did the drive by shooting. Mr. Thomas give me a couple of days; I'm going to step up the effort. I promise you I'm going to find that gang and bring them to justice."

"I sure hope you find them soon," said Rufus.

"Mr. Thomas, I'll let you know the minute anything turns up." After Lt. Elder hung up, Rufus decided to call his friend Leroy Jackson.

The phone rang about three times, then a female voice said,

"Hello."

"Hello Pat. This is Rufus. Is Leroy in?"

"Yes, he's out back. Hold on, I'll go get him."

After about a minute a male voice said, "Hello."

"Hello Leroy, this is Rufus, how are you today?"

"I'm doing pretty good. I was out back doing some work on my lawn mower."

"That damn gang struck again last night," said Rufus.

"What happened?"

"They spray painted and scrawled racial graffiti all over my building."

"That's terrible," said Leroy.

"I called Lt. Elder, and he promised me he was going to step up the effort and catch this gang and bring them to justice."

"I know you will be glad," said Leroy.

"You know Leroy, I've already written one letter to the editor, and I'm going to write another one today."

"Rufus, do you really think it will make any difference?"

"Leroy, I think it will. I'm saying things that somebody needs to say about all of this big government and the welfare state."

"Ain't nothing going to change," said Leroy.

"Leroy, I believe somebody must speak out on the destruction that is being done to this country.

I've decided to write a book about the dangers of the welfare state and social spending."

"Who are you going to get to publish it?" asked Leroy.

"I don't know, I may have to publish it myself. By the way Leroy, would you like to go fishing with me this Saturday evening at Grassy Pond?"

"Yes, I don't have any other plans."

"Good, I'll leave the restaurant early and let Erica and Zaporia close up. Leroy, I see some customers coming in, got to go now, I will talk to you later."

CHAPTER 3

On this Friday morning Loco Harris settled in his chair near the Christian retirement group. Reverend Whitehurst said,

"Loco, what religion are you today?"

Loco replied, "Guys, I first must stress that I'm not really a religious man anymore. Everything I tell you is strictly from a secular point of view. I must say that I do believe in a divine power, or superior being. You can call him God or whomever."

" How can you believe in God and not obey the bible?" said Deacon Jones. Loco didn't answer the question.

"You see," said Loco, "The countries of India and China, both with populations over a billion people contain major religions with more than one God. The main religion in China is Buddhism, and the main religion in India is Hinduism."

"You call them religions, as far as I'm concern those people are all going straight to hell," said Deacon Bines.

Loco ignored the comment and continues with his lecture, "No matter what religion one is they all stress avoiding thinking only of oneself. One needs to believe in something bigger than himself. As a rule the less selfish one is the more thankful, contented, and happy one is.

"If one's life is unhappy and unfulfilled, the secret is to serve God and do for others. The biggest secret to happiness of all is to treat all people as well as you would like to be treated, no matter how they treat you in return. The downside to that is it is extremely hard to treat someone well that treats you badly, but the few that truly can, reaches a spiritual plateau unsurpassed. The few that can truly refuse to hate their enemies reaches a supernatural spiritual peace that nothing can take away.

"From a spiritual point of view if you speak to someone and he won't speak back, don't feel insulted or angry, the problem is with him, not with you. In order to remain a good and decent person you must try to handle every situation in a good and decent manner. Over time one mean and unfriendly individual can make you just like him if you play the tit for tat game. Lastly, there is the old biblical truth that we reap what we sow."

LaTonya couldn't wait to get home to watch her favorite soap opera, "As The Earth Spins." She had helped her aunt Regina at her cafe all morning. She knew Bruce was probably playing basketball most of the day at one of the basketball courts in the Jimmy Carroll Housing Projects.

A dilemma was haunting her on whether to tell Bruce that Boom Boom had made a pass at her. Boom Boom had come on to her that morning at Regina's Cafe. Boom Boom had told her that he didn't know what she saw in Bruce; why didn't she give a real man a chance. Like himself. She told Boom Boom she wouldn't have anything to do with him if he was the last man on earth.

She knew if she told Bruce there would be a fight or even worse. She prided herself on being able to handle men. She reasoned that unless Boom Boom became too persistent or started harassing her, she would just keep quiet on the whole matter. She had told Bruce that she should be home by two o'clock

After playing basketball most of the day, Bruce checked his Timex. It was two thirty; he figured LaTonya should be home by now. He told his teammates that would be his last game.

Bruce said farewell to the guys and left walking to LaTonya's house. Bruce thought back to last Monday night. He would like to scare the old stooge that runs the Harlem Garden Restaurant off that property, but he didn't want to kill him.

He had decided to spray paint the racial graffiti on that building to keep up the pressure. With the neighborhoods changing all around a lot of the older business owners had already been scared off because of the high crime rate. He still believed that with enough pressure, the Harlem Garden Restaurant owner would pull out too.

As LaTonya's house came into view, Bruce thought LaTonya was a nice catch. Even with two kids, she almost graduated from high school. She often talked about getting her high school G.E.D.   Bruce was sure she was going to do it too. He had made it to the tenth grade, but by all practical means he had quit school.

Being only sixteen, he couldn't marry her now even if she would agree to marry him. He had nothing to offer her.   He couldn't take care of her. He felt fortunate because he was sure LaTonya loved him. He felt some way, somehow he would someday marry her. He would buy her a car, jewelry, furs and other nice things. She was about five eight and weighed around one hundred and forty lbs. with a superb figure. She was very neat and clean. She tried to hide it, but he knew secretly she was very ambitious.

He knew she would never stay on welfare very long. Deep down, Bruce sometimes wondered why she put up with him.

He decided she really did love him. Bruce smiled as he reached out to ring her door bell. He noticed one of the curtains being pulled to one side immediately after that, LaTonya opened the door. "Hello, LaTonya," said Bruce.
"Hello, Bruce, are you doing all right today?"
" I'm doing pretty good." LaTonya stood to the side as Bruce strode into the living room. He sat on the sofa and LaTonya came over and sat beside him. Bruce gave her a long French style kiss. "How did your day go, LaTonya."
"It went okay, how about yours?"
"I played basketball in the projects most of the day."
"Bruce, your mother thinks you are attending school. Good as you play basketball, you should go to school and play on the varsity. I'm sure you could get a scholarship to go to college."
"I don't know, LaTonya," said Bruce.
"Bruce, I've already started studying for my high school G.E.D. I hope to test before the end of the year, and if I pass I plan to enroll at Buieville Community College around the first of next year. I plan on getting my L.P.N. Degree."
Bruce leaned over and started French kissing her. Between kisses she whispered to Bruce, "My mother is keeping the kids, we have the whole afternoon to ourselves."

Friday morning Lt. Elder had planned on staying in his office and catching up on his paper work. Around eight thirty, his secretary, Carolyn Laverne, brought him a list of all the cars that had been stolen and recovered within the last two weeks.
On the list was a gray Honda Accord. He immediately picked up the phone and dialed Captain Eric Boyd, in charge of the Traffic Division.
"Hello, this is Captain Boyd Traffic Division."

"Eric, this is Marvin Elder over in the Youth Gang Division. I need some information on a gray Honda Accord that was stolen and recovered last week."

"Sure Marvin, I remember the car. We lifted several sets of fingerprints of that car. Let me transfer you to Mrs. Veronica Register, she will give you all the information we have on it."

"Hello, this is Mrs. Register, may I help you?"

"Yes, this is Lt. Elder over in Youth Gang Division. I need some information on a gray Honda Accord that was stolen and recovered last week."

"Just a minute, Lt., I need to bring up that file on the computer. Okay, what do you need to know?"

"First, I would like to know where was it stolen from."

"It was stolen from Eugene Sharpe's used car lot."

"Where was it found."

"It was found on Sirmans' Drive near the Jimmy Carroll Housing Projects."

"Thank you very much, Veronica, I believe that's all I will need. Hold it," said Lt. Elder, "just one last thing, do you know who found the car?"

"Yes, a young patrolman named Douglas Roosevelt on the graveyard shift. That's Captain Anthony Fuller's shift."

"I'm sure that will do it, Veronica, have a nice weekend."

"Same to you Lt." After hanging up, Lt. Elder thought about where the car was found. In almost all cases wherever a stolen car is found, the culprit or culprits live in that general area. He would ask his information sources the names of all gangs operating in and around the Jimmy Carroll Housing Projects. Lt. Elder decided instead of waiting until Monday he would go down to the Jimmy Carroll Housing Projects and see if he could find Littlejohn.

He knew Littlejohn could give him a list of the gangs operating in that area. He grabbed his portable and decided to leave for the Jimmy Carroll

Housing Projects. "Carolyn;" said Lt. Elder to his secretary, "I shouldn't be out of the office very long, I'm going out to the Jimmy Carroll Housing Projects."

"Yes sir."

"I have my portable with me in case I have to be located in an emergency."

"Yes sir."

When Lt. Elder arrived at the projects he decided to park near the office building as usual. He was hoping since it was before noon Littlejohn would still be home. He walked up to Littlejohn's front door and gave about three knocks. After a few seconds he heard movement inside.

"Who is it?" came a voice from inside.

"Lt. Elder."

"Just a minute." After what seemed like a full minute, Littlejohn opened the door.

Lt. Elder strode past him into the living room. "Littlejohn, I was hoping you would be in, I won't take but a few minutes of your time."

"Okay," said Littlejohn.

"Littlejohn, I have reason to believe the gang I am looking for is in this area." Lt. Elder got out his notepad and said,

"Littlejohn, I need the names of every gang operating in this area."

"There is a Latin gang, but I can't remember its name. There is the Young Vipers, and a little farther south is the Bonehead gang."

"How about the other gang, the Young Vipers?"

"The Young Vipers are mostly kids Lt. Some of them are as young as twelve or thirteen. The leader Bruce Allen is real mean, but seems to have some honor about himself. The real valueless one is his second in command Boom Boom. Boom Boom is the type that will take both your money and your life and feel no remorse."

Lt. Elder reached into his left pocket and pulled out a clip of bills, slid off five twenties and thanked Littlejohn.

43

"One other thing Littlejohn, where can I find Bruce Allen and the other leaders. Where do they hang out?"

Littlejohn thought for a minute. "Lt. there are two places Bruce Allen likes to hang out. Almost everyday, sometimes during the day, you will find him playing basketball on one of the courts here in the projects. The other place he like to hang out at is, Regina's Cafe down on S. Mary Alice Ave."

On his way back to his office Lt. Elder decided he would wait until Monday to follow up on those names. He believed one of those gangs was the one he was looking for.

Saturday, Rufus told Erica to close up the restaurant. He was taking off early to go fishing. At home, Rufus was deciding on what gear and fishing equipment to use. He decided to take along his spinning reel just in case the biting was slow. Then he might decide to do a little casting for bass using plastic worms. But today, he planned on fishing for bream or blue gill, a very good pan fish.

Rufus decided to use a light limber eight-foot long bamboo cane pole. That would allow him very good wrist action to pitch his bait from spot to spot while the boat slowly trolled the lake. The minute he got a bite, he would quietly anchor down.

If he didn't continue getting bites, he would start back trolling.

He decided on a number five blue steel hook that would bend without breaking.

He also decided to use a fifteen pound test line with a B.B. shot lead weight, about six inches from the hook and use a small slim line cork so there would be very little resistance when the fish bit and pulled on the hook. He also decided he would take along both crickets and red wigglers for bait. Finally, making sure there were at least two safety vests on board, he decided to give the fifteen foot bass master one last going over. Then he hooked her up to the Silverado.

Before leaving his house, he called Leroy to let him know that he was on his way. After leaving Leroy's house, they pulled into Alfred Myers Bait and Tackle Shop. They each purchased about fifty crickets and a small container of red wigglers. Now, finally, they were on their way. As he turned into the Old Stockton Road leading out of the city, Rufus smiled to himself and wondered if Sarah Whitlock still lived on this road.

He remembered years ago she was his first employee at the Harlem Garden Restaurant. She fell in love and married a rich undertaker, then he made her quit to take care of their eventually ten kids. They used to live in a nice colonial style home with bay windows on this road. He watched Leroy light up and take a long drag on his cigarette.

He often thanked God he found the strength several years ago to quit that costly stupid health snatching habit. But he guessed we all have a weakness for something.

"Leroy," said Rufus, "what do you think about people always complaining that they can't find any jobs?

"I don't think there are very many good jobs left," said Leroy, "all we got is jobs flipping hamburgers or some other minimum wage job.

"What I really think," said Rufus," is all of this crying about no jobs is a red herring or some other phony excuse. Just think about it, we have millions of illegal aliens in this country easily finding work. But somehow, poor Americans can't find work.

The availability of hard, tough work is the bait that is drawing the illegals to this country. If it was not for our welfare state, those now on welfare would have to do hard tough work, and there would be no jobs left to draw millions of illegals to this country. As for those minimum wage jobs, I have worked them and feel that anyone that has to work will take any job he can get until he can do better.

"One other thing is, this complaining about rich people making money. Attacking the rich is the first thing a dictator or socialist does. They try to falsely blame the rich for all shortcomings. That way they can distract and mislead the uninformed, while they promote their own power grabbing agenda. Balance is the key. We need a strong middle class.

Nobody poor is going to give anybody a job, so it stands to reason the more rich people we have and produce the more jobs we all will have. You can't get blood out of a turnip. Somebody has to have money to pay those that don't have any, otherwise nobody will have money to pay those that don't have any, like in a socialist system."

"Rufus," said Leroy, "don't miss your turn, next right."

"Okay, I won't. Let me say this last thing and I'll get off this subject. There is no shame in doing hard, tough work as long as one has the freedom and opportunity to better himself. But we will never get Americans to do hard, tough work as long as we have a welfare state like ours. There will always be some excuse not to work."

As they were pulling up to Grassy Pond, Leroy said, "I sure hope we catch a big mess of fish. There is nothing better on a Saturday night than a big bowl of cheese grits, coleslaw, sliced onions, deep fried fish, and hush puppies."

Once they got the fourteen foot bass master unloaded, they decided to slowly troll around the east side of the lake first.

They decided to start off using cricket first. Rufus took the front seat. He positioned the foot pedal for comfort to best guide and direct the boat. As the bass master named Yvette slowly eased through the water, Rufus used a slight wrist action with his light eight foot pole to pitch his cricket from one spot to the next.

They were about a hundred yards out in the lake when all of a sudden a blue gill hit his bait so hard his bamboo cane pole bent almost to the breaking point. As Rufus finally snatched the blue gill out of the water and let the fish slowly swing back to his open left palm, he then eased it into the live-well. One of the challenges of bringing in a big blue gill is they will turn sideways on you, then a pound and a half fish will pull like an five pound bass.

"Leroy," said Rufus softly, "ease out the anchor." When Rufus snatched the blue gill out of the water, he saw a clear, watery liquid streaming from the fish. He knew instantly this was their lucky day.

He realized it must be a full moon and the fish were on bed, meaning the fish would be in large groups and the males would be fertilizing the female eggs. He knew if it was a big bed they could catch their allotted amount in short order, because on a bed, you can catch them as fast as you can bait up. Unfortunately, it was a small bed.

They caught about ten blue gills as fast as they could throw out. Then nothing for the next fifteen minutes. It was not long before they found another bed. After being on the pond for a little over two hours, they had their allotted catch, then they headed for home. Once Rufus had dropped Leroy and his share of the fish off, he eased the Silverado back into traffic for the twenty minute drive to his home.

As the Silverado droned on, Rufus thought back to when he was a young petty officer in the U.S. Navy stationed in San Diego. Their daughter Freddy Mae was born after he and Janet had been married a little over a year. Both parents doted on their only daughter.

She was taught to be responsible for her actions. She was taught to treat all people well and decently as she would like to be treated no matter how she was treated in return, but always defend herself and not take any abuse. She was taught to always look for a reason to succeed instead of accepting any excuse for failure.

His mind came back to the present as Debra Marie Drive loomed into view. As he turned onto Debra Marie Drive, Rufus smiled to himself and decided he would call his daughter when he got home. Rufus put away his boat and secured everything.

He decided to clean just enough fish for a good meal. The rest make y of the fish he placed in two one gallon plastic milk containers with the top cut off them. He then filled them with water, and placed them in the freezer. He would clean the rest later as needed.

That night, he and Janet enjoyed a supper of cheese grits, coleslaw, sliced raw onions, dill pickle, deep fried fish, and hush puppies. Afterwards, they cuddled together on the sofa in the den, and viewed one of the latest video movies.

"By the way, Janet," said Rufus, "I have managed to finish writing two chapters in my book. I have also decided on a name for it. The name will be "Why We Must Dismantle The Welfare State," by Rufus Thomas.

CHAPTER 4

It had been quite awhile since Loco had eaten breakfast at the Harlem Garden Restaurant. After Loco had settled comfortably at his usual table, one of the Christian retirement group members said, "Hey Loco, are you a Hindi today?" They knew that would launch Loco on one of his lectures. After several seconds Loco replied, "You know, way back around 1500 BC the Hindu religion was born in India.

"Hinduism is a very old religion and it has had a big influence on many other religions over the years. Hinduism is a major world religion, and it is estimated to have more than 700 millions followers, mostly in India. Like most eastern religions, Hinduism regards more of what people do rather than what they think.

"It focuses mainly on rules for behavior and conduct. They acknowledge the existence of many gods, but most individuals are primarily devoted to a single God or Goddess. Most westerners know that they have a reverence for Brahmans and cows that prohibits them from eating beef. Their main text or authority is the Vedas.

"I still say that is a lot of soul being lost," said Reverend Whitehurst. cause

"Amen," said Deacon Jones.

LaTonya yelled at her two-year-old son because he was making too much noise banging a toy upside the wall. For Christ's sake, she couldn't hear what Karen Parker was saying on her favorite soap opera, "As The Earth Spins." She checked the time; it was almost noon. She decided to boil some wieners. Her boyfriend Bruce should be over soon and he might be hungry.

That reminded her to check her food stamps; the baby was almost out of milk. She would get Bruce to run to the store and get some milk and Fruit Loops. She put the wieners on slow cooking and returned to the sofa to watch her soap. As she watched the beautiful Asia Greene seduce her leading man on the, "Youth And The Reckless," she thought back to a couple of years ago when her stepfather had tried to rape her.

She had to go live in Miss Louise Gardner's Orphanage for young girls. Miss Gardner was very strict, but she was fair.

She taught her girls to believe in themselves, that they could be whatever they wanted to be. Someone knocking on her front door brought her back to the present. LaTonya walked over to the window and slightly parted the curtains to see who it was.

It was Bruce, and she immediately opened the door.

"Hello, LaTonya," said Bruce.

"Hello Bruce, how are you today?"

"Pretty good," said Bruce as he strode past her and sat on the living room sofa.

Bruce sat beside her on the sofa. He still found it hard to believe that he could hold on to a charming girl lIke LaTonya.

"Bruce," said LaTonya, "would you like for me to fix you a couple of hot dogs?"

"Yes, I would like a couple of hot dogs."

LaTonya got up walked over to the refrigerator and took out about three hot dog buns.

"Bruce, what would you like on your hot dogs?"

"Just ketchup and mustard will be fine."

LaTonya finished Id go fixing the hot dogs and brought them and a soda to Bruce on the sofa.

"Bruce, when you finish eating I would like for you to go to the store and get me some milk, and Fruit Loops for the kids."

"Okay, LaTonya, I'm going to leave early today. My mom told me to be home when she got off from work. She wants to have a very important talk with me." After eating his hot dogs, Bruce left for the nearest Flash Food Minute Market about a block away.

It took him about thirty minutes to return from the Minute Market. LaTonya made her two kids take their daily nap, then she took Bruce's hand and gently led him to her bedroom.

Later, as they lay talking she asked Bruce to please get out of the gang and go back to school. Bruce said he would think about it. Bruce checked his Timex. "LaTonya," said Bruce, "it is almost five o'clock I really must go. I will try to come over later tonight."

"Okay, I will get up and walk you to the door."

When Bruce got home, his two sisters, Tasha age fifteen and Tameka age fourteen were doing their homework. His mom was in the bathroom. Bruce sat on the living room sofa and started watching TV. After about fifteen minutes, Bruce's mother Miss Gracie Bell Allen came out of the bathroom.

"Tasha," yelled Ms. Gracie Bell, "is Bruce home yet?"

"Yes maam, he's watching TV in the living room."

"Bruce," yelled Miss Gracie Bell, "I want to talk to you in your room."

"Yes maam." As Bruce ascended the stairs to his room, he wonders what it was that his mother wanted to talk to him about that seemed so important.

He decided to himself that the jig was up; he was busted.

He knew it had to be about him playing hooky from school. As his mother stood by his room door, he strode past her into his room and sat on the side of his bed. His mother followed him into the room and closed the door. "Bruce," said Miss Gracie Bell, "I want the truth. I don't want to hear any lies. I want to know have you been going to school every morning when you leave here?"

Bruce thought about lying but sensed that his mother already knew the truth. After taking longer than necessary to answer, Bruce finally said, "No maam."

"Where have you been going every school day?"

"I've been playing basketball here in the projects and going to a friend's house."

"Who is this friend that you have been going to his house instead of going to school?"

"It is a she."

"I see," said his mom. "What is her name?"

"LaTonya Smith."

"How old is she?"

"She just turned eighteen."

"I want to find out more about this LaTonya woman, but that can wait. It was late when you got home last night, and I decided to wait until I got off work today to talk to you. The high school principal's office called me yesterday afternoon, and we had a long talk concerning you. They think you are headed for serious trouble. They think you not only skip school, but you are also involved in gang activity.

51

They feel it is only a matter of time before you will be dealing hard drugs. Bruce, I brought you into this world, and damn it, I will take you out of it.

"Bruce, I have made my share of mistakes, but I will not stand for this. I promise you if you stay in this house, you are going to school. Tomorrow, I'm going out to the school and talk to the principal. I'm going to tell her the first day of school you miss I want to know about it. I may have to send you to live in the country on your Uncle Hoover Charles' farm, but you can rest assured that if you skip school again there will be severe consequences. Do you understand me, young man?"

"Yes maam."

Monday morning Lt. Elder had already decided to bring in the leaders of two gangs. He decided to go after the Young Vipers first. The leaders of the Young Vipers were a sixteen- year-old name Bruce Allen, and another sixteen-year-old that went by the name Boom Boom. Lt. Elder knew he may need extra help in making this bust just in case things turned sour. Lt. Elder decided two other sergeants in the youth gang division may not be enough manpower.

He decided to bring in four additional uniformed officers for back up. One of the uniformed officers was a tough battle scarred chap named Lt. Joe Walsh. The other uniformed officers were Staff Sergeant Roger Miller, Corporal Dana Mitchell, and Corporal Charlie Johnson. Lt. Elder had the names of the gang leaders, but he didn't have the slightest idea how these kids looked.

He already had his task force organized and ready to move, but since he didn't know how these kids looked he needed to do a little leg work first. He had already gotten permission from Police Chief Jimmy Sampson to exempt members of his task force from other duties. The Young Vipers were reported to hang out at Regina's Cafe.

Lt. Elder told his secretary to log him out to Regina's Cafe and from there to the Jimmy Carroll Housing Projects. He should be back in a couple of hours. It was around nine thirty when Lt. Elder entered Regina's Cafe. There were no customers around at the time. The cooking area was behind the counter and about midway behind the counter, was a big, black eight burner gas stove with a large, smooth iron grill on the left and a large baking oven on the right.

At the far end of the counter toward the back of the diner, was what looked to be a storage room and office. Two women, who looked to be in their early thirties, seemed to ignore him and continued with their chores. Clearing his throat, Lt. Elder said, "I would like to speak to the owner."

"I am," said the lady nearest to him with a pleasant voice and ready smile as she turned around to face him. "I'm Miss Felicia Regina, owner of this establishment."

"I'm Lt. Elder from Buieville P.D." as he flashed his badge.

"Miss Regina do you know a sixteen-year-old by the name of Bruce Allen?" I have information that he and his friends come in here often.

Miss Regina looked in the direction of her employee, Miss Anna Ruth Leonard. "Anna Ruth, ain't that the name of the young man that be talking to my niece?"

"I do believe it is, Miss Regina."

"Lt. I do believe I know the young man, what he done?"

"We just need to ask him some questions," said Lt. Elder.

"How about the name Boom Boom; do you know him?"

"I don't think so." "

"Well, he's Bruce Allen's right hand man and is with him most of the time."

"You're right Lt.; the same one or two friends are with him almost all the time."

"Miss Regina, do you have a phone in the back where there is privacy?"

"Yes, I have one back in my office."

"Miss Regina, I would like to ask a favor of you. You don't have to do it if you don't want to."

Lt. Elder reached in his shirt pocket and pulled out a card.

"This is the number you can reach me," he said as he handed Miss Regina his card. "I would like for you to give me a call if Bruce Allen or any of his friends come in here today. Remember you don't have to do this if you don't want to."

"I'll give you a call Lt."

"Make sure you use the phone in back because the call must be in complete privacy. Also, make sure you describe the color and type of clothes they are wearing. Before I go, may I use your phone?"

"Sure Lt., come on around behind the counter," as she led him back to her office. Lt. Elder called his secretary and told her to contact him immediately on his portable if he got a call from Regina's Cafe. It was almost ten thirty when Lt. Elder arrived at the Jimmy Carroll Housing Projects.

He parked in the office parking lot as usual and made his way to Littlejohn's apartment. Once inside Littlejohn's apartment, Lt. Elder asked him if he could identify Bruce Allen and Boom Boom.

"Sure, I can identify both of them," said Littlejohn. "I see Bruce Allen playing basketball here in the projects almost every day. Boom Boom don't care as much for basketball, but he do be on the side line watching most of the time."

"What I would like for you to do, Littlejohn, is monitor all of the basketball courts here in the projects and the minute Bruce Allen or Boom Boom shows up give me a call. Since I don't know how he looks, make sure you give a good description of the color and type of clothes they will be wearing." Lt.

Elder reached in his shirt pocket and pulled out one of his cards, then reached in his left trouser pocket and pulled out a money clip, slid off a couple of twenties and thanked Littlejohn. Lt. Elder returned to his office and decided to catch up on his paper work while he wait on the expected calls.

It was almost one o'clock when Lt. Elder received the call from Regina's Cafe. Miss Regina told Lt. Elder that two of Bruce Allen's friends were in her place of business. They both looked to be around age sixteen and had on long shirts about three sizes too large. One of the shirts was gray with sea shell like designs, the other shirt was green with flowery designs.

"Okay guys," said Lt. Elder. "Let's go make this bust."

Lt. Elder and the other two plain cloths detectives from the Youth Gang Division rode in his unmarked sedan. Lt. Joe Walsh and the other three uniformed officers rode in two black and whites. Their instructions upon arrival was for the detectives to go in first and the uniformed officers to lag behind a little. When Lt. Elder pushed open the front door, he immediately spotted the two gang members. He cautiously approached their table and came to a stop directly in front of them. "Buieville P.D.," said Lt. Elder as he flashed his badge.

"Which one of you goes by the name of Boom Boom?"

"I do," said the youth in the gray shirt.

"I'm placing both of you under arrest for suspicion in a driveby shooting. You have the right to remain silent. Anything you say can and will be used against you in a court of law. You have the right to talk to a lawyer and have him present with you while you are being questioned. If you cannot afford to hire a lawyer one will be appointed to represent you before any questioning, if you wish one. Stand up, turn around, and place your hands behind your back." The two youths did as they was told and showed no resistance.

Both suspects were led outside and placed in one of the black and whites. Lt. Elder dismissed the other two sergeants from the Youth Gang Division plus one black and white and two corporals. He instructed Lt. Joe Walsh and the other uniformed officer in the black and white with the suspects to follow him. He wanted to stop by the Harlem Garden Restaurant on S. Mary Alice Ave.

About ten minutes after leaving Regina's Cafe, they arrived at the Harlem Garden Restaurant. After entering the restaurant, Lt. Elder asked the waitress out front to speak to Mr. Thomas.

The waitress went to the kitchen, and Mr. Thomas immediately came out front. "Hello, Lt.," said Mr. Thomas, "what can I do for you?"

"I have a couple of suspects of that driveby shooting outside.

I would like for you to come outside and see if they were the youths you ran off your parking lot."

"I would be glad to take a look." Lt. Elder led Mr. Thomas out to the black and white. Mr. Thomas leaned over to get a better view of the youths inside.

Then he walked a few feet away with Lt. Elder at his side. "The one in the gray shirt was definitely one of the kids I ran off my parking lot."

"Thank you, Mr. Thomas, we will take it from here." Lt. Elder took both youths back to the station for questioning. Boom Boom was told his fingerprints were found on the stolen car, but he denied any involvement in any driveby shooting.

He was sent to the district youth correction center in Belview, then two weeks later, he was sentenced to 4 months of boot camp. The other youth broke down during questioning and told everything and was released into the custody of his parents.

CHAPTER 5

After saying good morning on this Good Friday morning, Loco settled in his seat at his favorite table at the Harlem Garden Restaurant. Sometimes the Christian retirement group would engage Loco in just pleasant small talk and let it go at that. For a while it seemed like that was the way the morning would go, but then one of the group members just couldn't resist saying, " Loco, you must be a Buddhist today I suppose?"

"No, I am not," said Loco. " However, I must tell you that Buddhism also is a major world religion.

"There is estimated to be over 400 millions Buddhist followers world wide. Back in the 6th century BC in India they believed that over long cycles of time wisdom returned to earth and was given to a chosen individual, that person would be known as the Budda. In the 6th century BC in India, Siddhattha Gautama lived a life of leisure and pleasure because he was a member of a privileged and influential family.

"Just like today when there is very little challenge or struggle in one's life, it leaves a void. Gautama's life was unfulfilled, and he went in search to try to find meaning and purpose to his life. At that time in India the ascetic life was a long practice for those seeking a deeper meaning to life. Guatama had acquired five companions and followers in leading his ascetic life, but they deserted him when he decided to eat regularly.

"Gautama then spent a long time wandering alone. Then one day he seated himself under a large Bo tree by the side of the river. There he said a clear vision came to him. There he said the keys to life came to him. Then he arose to go teach his vision. He found his five former followers, and after five days he finally convinced them that he was now truly enlightened. They then shouted and proclaimed him as the Budda.

"The main points of Gautama's vision was that all miseries in life is because of selfishness, and greedy desires. Nirvana is the highest goal of the Buddhist path, an enlightened state when the desires of greed, hatred, and ignorance have been overcome. Buddhist are found mostly in Asia, but almost none in India where it was started.

"Buddhism has greatly evolved over the centuries. Several new sects developed in China. One of the sects most well known is Zen. Zen is the most popular sect found in the US."

Rufus decided he was not going to write a large book and that he would keep it down to around a hundred pages. He estimated he would be finished with his first draft in about another week. Since he identified one of the gang members for Lt. Elder, he felt finally this gang threat would soon be over.

He was in a good mood so he decided to do some writing on his manuscript.

He decided to write about one subject that he was truly sick and tired of. He was sick and tired of all this damn blaming everything and everybody but one's self in today's society.

You can talk to anyone successful, and he will tell you the key to success is to try and keep trying no matter the circumstances.

People that are always looking for something or somebody to blame are in his view irresponsible and dangerous. Just think about it, he thought, if one is independent and responsible he is not going to waste time blaming and depending on others. The surest proof of one's dependency and irresponsibility is wasting time and exercising in futility because someone doesn't like or accept him. It is irresponsible to waste time blaming others because they don't like you.

The fact is, if you are a good and decent person, good and decent people are going to accept you, otherwise they don't matter. Who cares so long as they can't hurt you. You can't make people like you if they don't want to, and it's dumb and shallow to think otherwise. The same people that are always blaming others are not doing a damn thing of substance for themselves or their fellow man.

All these years of welfare and social spending have conditioned far too many people to expect the government and others to do for them while they sit back and blame and complain. It has given far too many people a dependent mentality. They feel they are entitled to everything anybody else has without having to earn it. They try to blame and lay a guilt trip on others that prosper and earn their way instead of making their own actions produce worthy results.

It's a matter of focus. When a good ball team gets a bad call, it doesn't start focusing on the officiating but instead keeps its focus on its winning game plan. That is the same way it should be when dealing with racism. One should keep his focus on his goal and not lose focus on racism or anything negative.

It's impossible for racists or haters to destroy your mind unless you hate them back, then your own hate may end up consuming your mind and soul. If you get down into the gutter to settle a dispute with someone, there is no way to come out looking sparkling clean.

Sure, there is racism in this country, and I've faced it first hand, but my focus is on becoming as physically independent and self sufficient as possible. I for one don't fear racism because this country still offers me many options to become as good or successful as anyone. I'm not soft on racism.

I am completely against racism and bigotry in any form. It's just that we live in a real world and it is not wise to completely ignore human nature. The fact is, as long as different races are living among one another there is going to be some racism whether people admit it or not. Many of those complaining the loudest about racism are the biggest racists of them all.

It is short sighted for a minority race to be perceived or treated special in anyway, because it divides and turns other races against them. Things like affirmative action and hate crimes on the surface may seem helpful, but in the long run they divide and cause resentment among the races.

Sure, big government can protect us now, but nothing remains the same, and sooner or later the majority race is going to get its redress.

Racism will never keep a do-for-yourself person down when he has the freedom and opportunity like in this country.

All it is is another obstacle to overcome and overcoming obstacles is what makes successful people successful. The sensible thing is to concede racism, because as long as there are different races one will have to deal with it sooner or later.

Whether it is admitted or not, every race has its share of racists.

The solution is instead of all this blaming, we need more do- for-yourself Americans like in the days before the welfare state began. A do-for-yourself person is going to be more concerned about what he is going to do for himself than what somebody else may or may not do.

One other thing, when the liberals keep chanting let's put children first, let's put children first, let's put children first, they forget about the unborn aborted children. They were our future children too. To claim the government is responsible for our children is the main reason why our society is in a complete decline. Every individual parent is solely responsible for his or her own children, not the government , nor anyone else, unless the children are legally taken from the parent.

This whole government and society is on the brink of going bankrupt and breaking up like the former Soviet Union unless something is done to save our currency from becoming worthless from out of control spending. Still, you have shallow minded liberals demagoging the issue by hiding behind children. The sad fact is, if we don't start cutting spending and save this great nation nobody is going to be able to help the children or anybody. Sure, liberals care greatly about this nation and the things they advocate, but in most cases, their care is shallow and superficial.

Sixty years ago almost everyone was conservative because of the hardships and struggles to survive. Now, far too many people have become shallow with weak survival instincts, due to big government and social spending. It's a perception problem.

You can't get most people to see the value of self sufficiency and tough love in today's society. But, the facts are self sufficiency and tough love are survival tools that could save millions of lives if a severe calamity hit, and believe me, with the decline of our family and moral values this nation is becoming more and more vulnerable.

The best thing for a liberal is a little hardship and struggle that will wake him up and open his eyes. A little hardship and struggle will give a liberal some depth by sharpening his survival instinct. A weak survival instinct is why any society that has it too easy, will eventually destroy itself. There has to be some real, or imposed hardship and struggle in one's life in order to build good judgment and character.

Rufus checked his watch; it was well after five, so he decided he had better quit writing for now. He closed up the restaurant and went on home. On Friday nights, Rufus and Janet liked to attend all of their local high school home football games. Tonight, the Buieville Tigers were playing cross town rival, Hutto High Trojans at home.

It was around seven thirty on this clear fall night when Rufus and Janet left for the game. The sleek, new Towncar cruised through the silent, crisp cool South Georgia night air with the smooth grace of a champion race horse. They arrived at Lomax Field about ten to eight. That would give them ten minutes to settle in their seats before game time.

Tonight, the Buieville Tigers were facing undefeated cross town arch rival Hutto High Trojans. At half-time, the Tigers were up fourteen to seven. Late in the fourth quarter, the Tigers were down twenty to twenty-one with only fifteen seconds left in the game. On second and goal, the Tigers had just taken their last time out with the ball on the Hutto High Trojans' two yard line. Instead of kicking a field goal it appears the Tigers are going to run another play.

The referee windmills his hand to signal that time has started. The Tigers all state quarterback Hoover Sirmans II is under center. He drops straight back about five yards, he looks, he looks, he looks, ten, nine, eight, seven, six, all receivers covered, Sirmans zooms the ball over everyone's head out the back of the end zone. Three seconds left on the clock, the kicking team automatically runs onto the field.

Both teams are set. The kick holder gives the signal. The hike is good. The kick holder places the ball. The soccer style kicker follows through and keeps his head down, never looking up until he hears the roar of the crowd, then he is literally mobbed. There is sheer pandemonium as the home crowd goes wild.

Rufus still felt elated as he and Janet left the stadium and headed for home. "Janet," said Rufus, "I feel like celebrating a little, how about us stopping by the Dairy Queen for some ice cream?" "That would be nice, Rufus, I believe I will have a banana split." There was no line so Rufus was able to drive straight up to the drive-in station.

"May I help you?" said the speaker at the drive-in station.

"Give me a large cup of ice cream with nuts on top and a banana split," said Rufus.

"Will that be all sir?"

"Yes."

"That will be three seventy five, drive around please."

Rufus received his order, paid his bill, and headed for home.

After arriving home, Rufus and Janet sat on the sofa in the den.

Rufus put on some soft oldies music and they enjoyed their ice cream. Later they fell asleep in each other's arms after n some consummating the night in perfect bliss and ecstasy.

Around three thirty, Lt. Elder and the other officers were still on alert static. "Lt. Elder, Littlejohn on line two," said his secretary Carolyn Laverne.

"Lt. Elder speaking."

"Lt. I have bad news, I can't figure it out, Bruce Allen is always playing basketball everyday here in the projects. I don't know what happened, but I haven't seen him all day."

"Littlejohn," said Lt. Elder, "you can call it a day. I appreciate the effort you gave it."

After hanging up from talking to Littlejohn, Lt. Elder decided he was going to release most of the task force. He decided to hold over two of the uniformed officers, Lt. Joe Walsh and Corporal Dana Mitchell. Everyone else was dismissed. During questioning, they managed to get some crucial information out of the youth with Boom Boom.

They know where Bruce Allen lives, where he supposedly went to school, where his girl friend lives, etc. After releasing the other members of the task force, Lt. Elder in his sedan and the two uniformed officers in their black and white, headed for Bruce Allen's home in the Jimmy Carroll Housing Projects. It was after four o'clock when they arrived at Bruce Allen's address.

Lt. Elder and the other two uniform officers walked up to Bruce Allen's apartment. Lt. Elder pulled the screen door back and gave three loud raps.

"Who is it?" said someone from the inside.

"The police."

A wide eyed girl opened the door immediately.

" Does Bruce Allen live here?" said Lt. Elder.

"Yes sir."

"We would like to talk to him."

"He ain't home."

"Do you know where we can find him?"

"No sir." long

As Lt. Elder and the officers walked back to their cars, "Joe," said Lt. Elder, "school has already turned out for the day. The most likely place he will be is at his girl friend's house."

Shortly thereafter they arrived at LaTonya's home on Cummings Street. As the officer's approached LaTonya's front door, Lt. Elder instructed Corporal Mitchell to go around to the back door just in case Bruce tried to skip out. When Lt. Elder knocked on the front door, they noticed a curtain near the door part slightly. Within a few seconds, a young lady opened the door about eight inches.

Past her, Lt. Elder could see a young man sitting on the sofa.

"Is Bruce Allen here," said Lt. Elder?

The young lady just stared at him for several seconds.

Finally, she said, "Yes, he is here."

"We would like to talk to him."

LaTonya opened the door wide and stood aside. Lt. Elder and Lt. Joe Walsh entered the living room.

"Are you Bruce Allen?" said Lt. Elder to the young man sitting on the sofa.

"Yes sir, I am," said Bruce Allen.

"I am placing you under arrest as a suspect in a driveby shooting. You have the right to remain silent. Anything you say can and will be used against you in a court of law. You have the right to talk to a lawyer and have him present with you while you are being questioned. If you cannot afford to hire a lawyer one will be appointed to represent you before any questioning, if you wish one. Stand up, turn around, and place your hands behind your back." Bruce Allen did as he was told and offered no resistance.

Lt. Elder used his car phone to call Rufus Thomas at the Harlem Garden Restaurant, but he didn't get an answer. He then called Mr. Thomas' home and his wife said he hadn't arrived from the restaurant yet. Lt. Elder left word for Mr. Thomas to call him at his office as soon as he got home. Back at the station, Lt. Elder questioned Bruce Allen about his involvement in the driveby shooting on the Harlem Garden Restaurant.

Bruce Allen denied any involvement in the driveby shooting or the spraying of graffiti. Around five thirty, Rufus Thomas called. Lt. Elder asked him if he would come down and identify another youth that he believed was involved in the driveby shooting. Mr. Thomas said he would be there in about thirty minutes. Lt. Elder also called Bruce Allen's mother and informed her of the trouble Bruce was in. She said she would be down right away.

Upon arrival at the station, Rufus Thomas told the desk sergeant why he was there. The desk sergeant paged Lt. Elder to the front desk. "I'm glad you could come down, Mr. Thomas," said Lt. Elder as he approached the front desk.

"I'm more than glad to do whatever I can to help bring these criminals to justice."

"Come with me, Mr. Thomas," said Lt. Elder as he led him to a viewing room that was behind a two way mirror.

Once inside the viewing room, Lt. Elder told Mr. Thomas to see if the youth in the other room was one of the youths he ran off his property.

"That's him," said Mr. Thomas, "that's the one that did the talking."

"Are you absolutely sure," said Lt. Elder.

"Without a doubt in my mind."

"Thank you very much, Mr. Thomas, you can go now."

Lt. Elder led him back to the front desk. "Thanks again, Mr. Thomas, for coming."

"You're welcome."

After Mr. Thomas' departure, Lt. Elder begin making arrangements to have Bruce Allen transported to the district youth correction center at Belview. Lt. Elder was paged to the front desk. He was sure it must be Miss Gracie Bell Allen, Bruce Allen's mother. "Hello, I'm Lt. Elder. Are you, Bruce Allen's mother?" asked Lt. Elder as he approached the front desk.

"Yes, I'm his mother." and I

"Miss Allen, we are sure your son is guilty. We have a witness and your son's fingerprints were found on the stolen car that was used in the driveby shooting. We cannot turn him loose in your custody. This evening he will be taken to the district youth correction center at Belview. Then in about two weeks he will go before a judge. Since this is his first arrest, the judge will probably sentence him to four months of boot camp instead of him facing a jury trial and receiving time in an adult prison. Come with me Miss Allen, you will be allowed a thirty minute visit."

After Miss Allen left and all arrangements had been made to transport Bruce Allen to Belview, Lt. Elder decided to go home; he still had time to make it to the Buieville High Tigers football game.

CHAPTER 6

Loco had enjoyed his breakfast and was sipping on his coffee when Deacon Bines said, " Loco, for the life of me I can't see how you can believe in God with all of that stuff you be talking."

After taking another sip of coffee Loco said, "Deacon this may not answer your question, but this is my basic outlook on the whole matter. I definitely believe in one God, or a superior being.

"I believe our creator gave us a brain equipped with reason and a logical thought process. This logic and reasoning is a mental box that we can't get out of. That is why we can't solve the old chicken and egg riddle. That is why we believe there has to be a beginning to everything no matter how far back. From a scientific point of view there is no beginning or ending because matter cannot be created or destroyed, only changed from one form to another. That says that what's here has always been here in some form, but logically speaking that's impossible, there has to be a higher level of reasoning ever u than logic to ever understand our existence.

"Man made computers and designed them on the binary base. It will never be able to count more than one or two at a time. Electronically speaking #1 may be a negative charge and #2 a positive charge. Then when this process takes place at lightning speed you have a super computer. Just like all computers are limited to the binary design, man's reasoning is limited to logic.

"Now, to change the subject, I'm going to speak from a purely secular point of view on religions. The invisible one God concept that is so reasonable that we take for granted today has not always been the case. In fact, almost all ancient civilizations had many gods and goddesses. The three dominant early civilizations of Egyptians, Greeks, and Romans all had many gods And goddesses.

Due to the Rosetta stone there is a written history long before the invisible one God concept. One of the early Egyptian Pharaohs was the first to promote the invisible one God concept, but like most things in ancient history, any new belief was seen as a threat. In those days they had a simple formula for dealing with threatening beliefs. Just kill everyone with the belief. The established Egyptian priests took that step, and thought that they had wiped the invisible one God concept off of the face of the earth forever. But, they were wrong, they didn't get everyone, because centuries later the invisible one God concept resurfaced full force among the Jews.

"Today the Jewish, Christian, and Moslem faiths with their belief in one invisible God are by far the dominant religions of the world Not including the Jewish and Moslem, there are over 2 billion Christians alone world wide. Most other religions of the world are mainly rules and guides for behavior and proper living, but especially the Christian faith with its power of the Holy Ghost, it really comes alive and stirs the soul."

Rufus took his spiritual life very seriously. Serving the Lord was a well established tradition in his family. His uncle was a preacher, and his father was a deacon. He also had a brother who was a minister and two other brothers who were deacons.

Growing up, Rufus didn't have a choice about going to church. His father's law was, "Me and my family will serve the Lord." As a young man, Rufus had sowed his share of wild oats, but even when young he had the sense to never experiment with drugs. Otherwise, he stayed out late, partied hard, and did a lot of things he shouldn't have. Old Prospect Baptist Church was the family church.

As young as he could remember as a boy, he had sat in the pews of the Old Prospect Baptist Church. While away in the navy he sort of backslid from his religious upbringing. Even back home out of the navy it was several years before he started back attending church regularly. Then about ten years ago, he became a deacon at Old Prospect Baptist Church. He also has been a Sunday school teacher almost as long.

On Sunday mornings, Rufus liked for Janet to fix him one of those old fashioned southern country breakfasts. She would fix homemade buttermilk biscuits, smoked sausage, Canadian bacon, grits, scrambled eggs, jelly, real butter, and orange juice.

After breakfast, they left for Sunday school. Their regular pastor would not be preaching today.

Today's guest speaker would be visiting pastor Rev. John B. Miley.

After the eleven o'clock service had started and Rev. Miley launched into his sermon, Rufus' mind drifted back to some of the great sermons his late cousin Rev. Robert Flagler of Fernandina Beach Florida used to preach. He remembered how Rev. Flagler stressed Philippians fourth chapter, thirteen verse, "I can do all things through Christ who strengthens me." He stressed how anyone down and out with little or no self confidence could repeat that verse over and over to himself at least fifty times a day, and it would guarantee him a successful life if only he kept saying it.

Here is another good positive saying to repeat fifty times or more each day to help one lose weight, "I'm going to have a slim body, soon." The mind tries to fulfill any image constantly presented to it. It doesn't matter whether it is real or imagined, positive or negative. The mind doesn't distinguish; it only recognizes images. That is why it is so important to think positively. That is why many of the old sayings have grains of truth in them, sayings like, "Out of sight out of mind," this can be a factor concerning sex education, and a scary man can't win in gambling or in battle.

The mind can't remember and deal with all of our experiences at once, so it tends to remember and act on the images that is presented the most constantly. The images that are presented less and less will soon be forgotten and not acted upon, but like in everything there are exceptions. For instance, in cases of trauma, an indelible imprint can be stamped in one's memory in a matter of seconds and last forever.

Another old saying used when someone was struggling with a problem was, "Go home and sleep on it." There is great benefit in that because it allows the subconscious mind time to help sort out and organize the problem. The mind receives so many conflicting images during a day that one would go crazy if the mind didn't use sleeping and dreaming as a sorting and filing process to organize recent images. Most of us are not aware of the negative thought images that we constantly feed our mind, but the good thing is we can make a conscious effort to think of positive images.

We have the ability to choose. One can decide how he will treat another human being no matter how that person treats him in return. The most powerful positive thinking image I know of is to love and forgive all people no matter how they treat you.

That doesn't mean you let anybody mistreat you. You always defend yourself from attacks. You can hate a person's ways and actions but still love the person as a human being.

There may be cases when someone is determined to make you hate him, then turn it over to God, just repeat to yourself, " I can wish all people goodwill, even if it's not returned." When you treat other people well, and they don't return the favor, you are not doing them a favor; you are doing yourself a favor, because as long as you treat all not d people well, you will stay a good person and mostly good things will happen in your life. Then nothing nor anybody can mentally defeat or destroy you.

You never see those who can genuinely love and forgive in mental wards, you won't see them as bums on the streets, or losers in any way. It is not enough to say I don't hate anybody, what really matters is how things are acted out. That means how you actually treat all people on a day-to-day basis. There is no way you can hate anybody, not even your enemy if you make it a practice to treat all people well like you would a loved one.

Sure, there is a need for hate and all emotions, but never hate anybody in your midst unless you are prepared and able to destroy them, lest they destroy you. The rule of thumb is to choose to treat all people well with courtesy and respect. When Rev. Miley's voice roared into one of those soul stirring hymns, it brought Rufus' mind back to the present.

After the service, Rev. Miley stood at the front door and shook the hands of the congregation as they filed out. In the Towncar on their way to Mitchell's Barbecue Restaurant for their Sunday dinner, Janet asked Rufus how he liked the sermon Rev. Miley preached.

"Rev. Miley preached a great sermon," said Rufus, "but to be frank I spent most of the time remembering some of the great sermons my late cousin Robert Flagler used to preach. My view on religion is I believe in God as much as anyone, but I also believe God helps those who first help themselves.

"I believe if you do as good as you can do or go as far as you can go, then some way, somehow God will help you go the distance. Otherwise faith without action is wasted."

They had a nice Sunday dinner of southern fried chicken, barbecue ribs, mustard greens, potato salad, macaroni and cheese, rice and gravy, sweet potato pie, corn bread, and iced tea.

Once back home Rufus decided to send out several queries to find a publisher for his almost completed book.

Bruce Allen had never seen his mother as angry and upset as when she found out he had not been going to school. No matter how much he thought that going to school was a waste of time, he knew he didn't have any choice because his mother was dead serious. The next day at school he felt out of place, but he knew he had to make the best of a bad situation.

Somehow, he got through his first day back.

He felt especially elated when the bell ring ended the school day. Not so much because school was letting out but because he was going to see LaTonya. He and LaTonya were watching TV when they heard someone knocking on her front door.

Race And Economic Problem Final Solution In USA

When Bruce heard someone ask for him with an unmistaken tone of authority, he knew instantly it was the police and he knew why they were there.

He knew it was too late to go out the back door because they had already seen him sitting on the couch. He knew there was no point in trying to resist, he might as well go quietly.

After being arrested and taken to the station, he was fingerprinted and booked. During questioning, he denied having anything to do with any driveby shooting. They claimed they lifted his fingerprints off of a gray Honda Accord that had been stolen the night of the driveby shooting.

Lt. Elder repeatedly asked him if he was in anyway involved in a driveby shooting. Each time they asked, he denied everything. Later, what bothered him most was the pain and hurt in his mother's eyes. He felt he had truly let his mother down. He loved his mother more than life itself. He decided then and there that if he ever got through this trouble he would swear before God to go straight, because never again would he put his mother through that kind of hurt and pain.

After he had told his mother how sorry he was for having hurt her, he then told her if the Lord got him through this, he would finish school and leave gangs and drugs behind. With tears in his eyes, he told his mother good by. Sergeant Victory Kocher, a young detective on the night shift, transported him the thirty miles to the district youth correction center at ht shi Belview.

At the center he was issued brogans, coveralls, underwear, tooth paste and tooth brush, and bed linen. The next morning he had to meet with the center's chief psychiatrist Doctor Zebedee Moore, then he had an appointment with the center's rehabilitated strong man, Chaplain David Taylor. He was assigned to dormitory "B." Each dorm was managed by a supervisor.

He was to report to his dorm supervisor any problems or criticism he had. He was told he would be there until his court date in about two weeks. Bruce was not used to being told everything to do, in fact he had never had any strict discipline, period. He managed to adjust to the regimental style of life better than he at first imagined. He had been at the center now for almost two weeks, and his court date would be coming up in a few days.

It's been almost two weeks now since Lt. Elder put those youth gang leaders behind bars. Rufus felt good about how his life was going at the present. Business was good at the restaurant. The gang problem had been taken care of. He had found a publisher for his book. So he decided he would celebrate by buying Janet a diamond ring.

Lee's Press, Inc. a small publishing company would be publishing his first book. The small publishing company couldn't promote it as much as Rufus knew it deserved, so he knew if the book was going to make it big he would have to do a lot of the promoting himself. He would try to get on the Frances Waddell talk show and as many talk shows as possible.

The publishing company was going to start off with sixty thousand copies for the first printing. They will give him two hundred copies to give to friends, do self-promoting, sell or do as he pleased. The publisher was going to run some ads in a few big city newspapers, but Rufus knew that for the book to sell he would have to make the rounds of talk shows and hustle his own book.

Juvenile Judge Fred Smith had very little sympathy for spoiled, ill-raised, undisciplined youngsters. He felt lack of discipline was the root cause of all the problems with today's youths. Most of the kids that come before him have never been conditioned to fear punishment or consequences.

Many of these kids have never heard a cold hard firm voice of authority demanding obedience. They look at him wide-eyed and bewildered when he chews them out.

Judge Smith knew that most of the kids that come before him would never be there if someone would have shown them love and put the fear of punishment and consequences in them the first time they broke the law. Most of the people running around talking about people being mean spirited are too shallow to see past their noses. They are hollering that conservatives don't have any compassion. They don't know what real compassion is. Real compassion is about protecting and saving the whole country, not about saving a few and letting the whole country perish and go to hell.

We all have a free will to adapt, but to waste compassion on those that choose not to adapt is not only a waste of time, it is dangerous. All animal or specie survival is dependent on their ability to adapt to their environment, otherwise they perish. Not forcing people to depend on themselves, their family, their extended family, their community, and private organizations is being weak, irresponsible, and negligent, not showing compassion.

It is always easier to be weak and take the course of least resistance, but in the end it will cost this country dearly if not destroy it. Real compassion is to be prepared to survive as an organized society under all conditions, even if the government goes broke and money becomes worthless. Trying to get liberals to understand that is like talking to a brick wall.

Those with the foresight and wisdom must speak out on the necessity of conditioning people to depend on each other as much as possible for their survival. No one knows how much time we have to prepare, but the destruction of moral and family values are always the last stage. Big government is the cause of the problem, not the answer.

Race And Economic Problem Final Solution In USA

Judge Smith knew he could save more of these youngsters if he could put the fear of God in them, thereby conditioning them to fear punishment and consequences.

Bruce didn't know what to expect as he sat in juvenile court that Monday morning when his name was called. His mother was sitting on his left, and uniformed officer Corporal Andrew Desantis was on his right. After his name was called, Officer Desantis escorted him to a rail about ten feet in front of the judge then left him alone and stood off to one side.

As Bruce stood there, the judge continued to read a report.

"State your name," said Judge Smith to Bruce in a loud, demanding voice.

"Bruce Allen, your honor" (as he had been coached).

"How do you plead to the charges?" said Judge Smith.

"Not guilty, your honor."

"We have an eye witness, and how did your fingerprints get on a stolen car that was believed to be used in the driveby shooting?"

"I don't know, your honor."

"Young man, you could go before a jury and be sentenced to several years of hard time in prison as an adult, but since this is the first time you have come before me, I am going to sentence you to four months of boot camp at Pine Valley Youth Correction Institution. But if you ever come before me again, young man you are going to be put away for a long, long time. Do you hear me young man?" said Judge Smith in a loud cold angry voice.

"Yes sir, your honor."

"Take him away, bailiff," said Judge Smith.

Bruce was allowed to say good bye to his mother and LaTonya. Then he was taken to boot camp at Pine Valley Correction Institution.

At Pine Valley everything was done in regimental style like in a real military boot camp. After arriving at Pine Valley, he was issued clothing and assigned a bunk in an open bay dormitory. Every morning they had to get up at five thirty.

They were given thirty minutes to make their beds with perfect hospital corners, brush their teeth, shave, shower, etc.. Breakfast was served from six to seven.

Calisthenics was from seven to nine. Classes and training were from nine to twelve. Lunch from twelve to one. Classes and training from one to four thirty. Dinner from four thirty to five thirty. Recreation and leisure time from five thirty to ten p.m.. At ten p.m. all lights out. Bruce was taught to say yes sir or no sir to every command or instruction. Some of the training instructors were retired military.

One of his instructors was a mean, tough, computer whiz named Sergeant Johnnie Roberson. Bruce remembers his first morning at reveille. They had to stand at attention while Sergeant Roberson walked up and down the line inspecting the prisoners. He stopped in front of Bruce and placed his face about four inches from his. "What is your name prisoner?" said Sergeant Roberson in a loud, angry voice.

"Bruce Allen, sir."

"I can't hear you."

"Bruce Allen, sir," said he in a loud voice.

"I still can't hear you."

"Bruce Allen, sir," said he almost yelling.

"Where you from prisoner?"

"Buieville, Georgia, sir."

"The only thing that comes from there is skunks and punks, which one are you prisoner?"

"Neither, sir."

"Are you calling me a liar prisoner?"

"No sir."

"I'm going to be watching you prisoner, and if I see you step out of line, your ass is grass and I'm the lawn mower, do you hear me prisoner?"

"Yes sir."

Sergeant Roberson took several steps backward, then he yelled out, "Column right, hut, two, three, four, hut, two, three, four," and on they marched to the dining hall.

At first, Bruce wanted to rebel and resist being told everything to do, but after a while he learned to control his anger and actions. Then for the first time in his life he felt a new power and control over his actions. He realized one's own actions determines the results one gets out of life. After more than a month at Pine Valley, Bruce knew that he was going to make it. He had gained enough self-control to do the right thing and stay out of trouble.

His mother and LaTonya visited and stood by him. The least he could do would be to stay out of trouble and not let them down.

CHAPTER 7

It's been almost a week since Rufus received his free two hundred copies of his first book, "Why We Must Dismantle The Welfare State By Rufus Thomas." Rufus had immediately started doing his share to promote his new book. He sent copies to all of the major book suppliers around the country.

He sent copies to all of the largest big city newspapers. He also sent copies to major public and college library systems around the country.

He requested to be on several talk shows. He offered to lecture and sign copies of his book at public functions, churches, prisons, etc. Within the next three months, he had invitations to appear on the Frances Waddell talk show and several other talk shows. Next month he was scheduled to speak at Pine Valley Youth Correction Institution.

Rufus had no intention of ever seeking public office himself, but if he could convince just one person in office of the dangers of big government and the welfare state, that alone would make it all worthwhile. The government has taken on a provider role and is saddled with huge financial burdens with millions and millions of people, some totally dependent on the government for their only survival. That is irresponsible and negligent for any free society to do, especially when the government doesn't have the self-discipline to control spending. What are all those people to do when the government goes broke? Only a fool will believe it can't happen.

It is obvious that it is only a matter of time before the debt gets so big the government can't raise taxes high enough, borrow enough money, or sell enough bonds to finance it.

Then the government won't have any choice but to print more and more money. After a while printing all of this money will cause hyper-inflation making the greenback practically worthless. With a very weak nuclear family and extended family system, this country could lose fifty million plus people and split along regional and ethnic lines. With our loose family and moral values, there is no solid foundation left to organize and rebuild upon. With money being worthless, there would be nothing the government could do without international help.

But if the dollar went down, it would probably bring the world economy down with it. The economy is already so distorted that our currency is like Monopoly money with the way sports figures and entertainers are being paid.

What are we to do, with the family and the extended family structure almost destroyed from fifty years of becoming dependent on an over generous, non-disciplining, and super rich sugar daddy government. On the other hand, when responsibility is passed to the states and local governments that should help rebuild the family foundation, then if the central government went broke, all would not be lost.

One month later Rufus was up, up, thirty three thousand feet into "The long, delirious burning blue," The wild blue yonder, "Where never lark, or even eagle flew," on his way to the Big Apple to appear on the Frances Waddell talk show. It was an all expense paid trip.

On the show, Rufus was asked how can you be so uncaring as to cut out school children's lunch program money?

"We have to ask ourselves this question," said Rufus,

"which is more important, to cause much hardship or lose the whole country? I say save the country first, then the children may have to take a lunch pail or bag to school or whatever is necessary. People will always find a way to survive on their own unless they depend on the government so long and forget how to do for themselves."

After returning to Buieville, Rufus enjoyed his new fame.

He and his book received a big write up in the "Buieville Daily Times." His publisher reported that his book was selling great.

At the rate they were selling, the initial sixty thousand would be sold out in two weeks. The publisher was already making preparations for a second printing.

Three weeks later Rufus spoke at Pine Valley Youth Correction Institution. Afterward he signed copies of his new book. As Rufus was signing books he was surprised and taken aback when Bruce Allen wanted Rufus to sign a book for him.

Rufus thought of his religious upbringing, he thought of a youth gone astray, and he thought of the power of forgiveness.

Rufus stared at the young man.

"Mr. Thomas," said Bruce Allen, "I'm sure you know who I am."

"I do?"

"If you find it in your heart to forgive me of the wrong I've done you, I just want you to know that I'm truly sorry."

"What are you going to do when you get out?" said Rufus.

"I promised my mom that I would finish school, sir."

Rufus thought that a young man living with his family in the Jimmy Carroll Housing Projects could use some pocket spending money. "I'll tell you what young man, if you are willing to work, come to see me at the restaurant when you get out." That night Rufus lay relaxing in bed after he and Janet had made love. "You know Janet," said Rufus "a strange thing happened to me today at my speaking engagement at Pine Valley Correction Institution. One of the youths convicted in the driveby shooting on my restaurant bought one of my books and wanted me to sign it. He told me he was sorry about what he had done. I not only autographed his book, I offered him a job when he gets out, but I can't help but wonder if I did a dumb thing."

"Honey, you've always enjoyed helping people. You wouldn't be happy any other way."

"I guess you're right, dear. Good night, darling," said Rufus.

After four months, Bruce had done his time and was let out of boot camp, but he still was on probation for another four years. Bruce was determined to keep his promise to his mom.

He decided to stay away from his old friends and the gang. He decided no matter what, he was going to finish school. He got word that Boom Boom had become leader of the Young Vipers. Bruce tried out for the Buieville High basketball team.

He not only made the team, he was going to be a starter.

His girl friend LaTonya had passed her high school G.E.D. and was scheduled to enroll at Buieville Community College the next quarter to get her L.P.N. degree. Three weeks later, Bruce and LaTonya were watching TV when the newscaster reported that a local gang leader who went by the name of Boom Boom was killed last night in a driveby shooting.

A few nights later Bruce was sitting with LaTonya on the sofa. "You know, LaTonya," said Bruce, "I stopped by the funeral home this afternoon to see Boom Boom, and deep down in my soul, I knew that the body lying there could just as easily have been me. Truly the Lord does work in mysterious ways," said Bruce. "At the time I thought being arrested was the worst thing that could have happened to me, but as it turned out being arrested and going to boot camp was actually the very best thing to ever happen to me. It gave me a second chance to live, and I'm going to make the best of it. Boom Boom blew his second chance, but not me."

"Honey, I am so proud of you," said LaTonya.

"Thank you dear, but I could never have done it without you and mom's support."

Rufus was back in the kitchen when Erica stuck her head in the doorway. "Mr. Thomas, there is a young man out here that says he would like to talk with you."

"Erica, tell him I'll be there in a minute." As Rufus pushed open the kitchen door he recognized the young man as Bruce Allen immediately. Rufus walked behind the counter to right across from where Bruce Allen was standing.

"Hello, Mr. Thomas," said Bruce Allen as Rufus came to a stop.

"Hello Bruce."

"Mr. Thomas, I came by to see if you are still willing to give me a job."

" We close around three thirty during the week, but we stay open to nine p.m. on Friday and

Saturdays, so I can let you come in for a twelve hour day on Saturday if you would like that."

"Yes sir, Mr. Thomas. I certainly would appreciate it."

"When would you like to start?"

"Quick as I can; this Saturday will be fine."

"Fine," said Rufus, "I will pay you minimum wage; be here at eight a.m. this Saturday."

"Yes sir, I'll be here, and thank you very much Mr. Thomas."

Rufus knew about fifty dollars wasn't a lot of money, but it would help teach the youth the work ethic and provide him with pocket money. After four Saturdays Bruce proved to be a dependable, willing worker. Rufus and Bruce sort of took to each other. Rufus never had a son and Bruce never had a dad; it seemed to be a perfect match. Already, Rufus had taken Bruce fishing in his boat, the first time Bruce had ever been fishing in his life.

Rufus hadn't seen Loco in quite a while, but sooner or later he always comes around. Detective Marvin Elder stopped by the restaurant often to chat a few minutes and have a cup of coffee with Rufus. Rufus' book had gone into its second printing. He couldn't judge how much effect his book had to do with the mood of the country, but he took comfort in observing the whole country going through a peaceful revolution.

Even the bleeding heart liberals were admitting something had to be done about the welfare mess. Only in the U.S. can a poor, shy country boy rise up and touch the heartbeat of America. Rufus decided to end his book by saying, God bless America.

THE END

SOME FINAL THOUGHTS

After reading this far, and everything is said and done, nobody is going to accomplish very much in life unless he has faith in himself. Everybody has a talent for something, and can do just about anything he makes up his mind to do. People like to complain, "I wish I could do this, or fix that," mostly things anybody can do, all they have to do is try.

The real secret in life is to be willing to try almost anything, no matter what it is. People are different. Some people learn quickly and others take a lot longer, but everybody can learn, if only they are willing to give it a try.

Many people just don't have the necessary faith that they can do anything they set their minds to. Believing one can do anything one sets one's mind to will automatically give one a I-can-do-for-myself-mentality, then one can do for oneself and not have to depend on anybody's goodwill for survival. The best faith builder I know of comes from the Bible.

All one has to do is use it as a positive thought; just repeat it to oneself at least 50 times a day, "I can do all things through God who strengthens me," and never quit saying it, because it really doesn't matter whether one believes it or not. It may take six months or longer, but sooner or later the faith will be there.

Still, there is the need and will to act because faith without action doesn't mean anything.

AUTHOR'S LONG BATTLE WITH NEUROSIS
April 06, 1999
Taking a quote from the old Negro spiritual, " Nobody knows the trouble I see, nobody knows my sorrows," I've decided to share this personal experience in hope that it may help someone else in his struggle. I'd like to share some positive saying quotes that I've used or created over the years.

The first one comes from the Bible. It gave me the confidence and faith to take on this battle and never give up. I would repeat fifty or more times a day, " I can do all things through God who strengthens me, "(paraphrased) Philippians 4:13.

As long as I can remember I've been shy and insecure, but mostly insecure. As an adult looking back, I believe getting whipped for wetting the bed as a child caused my neurotic symptom of looking pitiful. It was a kind of neurosis that would cause me to look pitiful in certain situations.

It was the only neurotic behavior I had to deal with the first twenty three years of my life. The symptom tended to kick in when I was exhausted or had to stand before large crowds. It would happen only if I thought about looking pitiful. But when

I played football and basketball in high school, my mind would be occupied and the neurotic symptom wouldn't occur.

Overall the problem was easy to deal with. I simply avoided standing before large crowds and would keep to myself when tired and exhausted. So, I just accepted my fate and enjoyed life. Plus, I had almost complete peace of mind.

Then at the age of twenty four all of that suddenly changed. A very strange and powerful neurosis invaded my mental concentration and robbed me of much of my peace of mind when in the company of other people.

It began after I returned home after four years in the military and started living with my parents again. When someone would sit beside me it would distract me and keep me from focusing and concentrating straight ahead. So, instead of having complete peace of mind and focusing one hundred percent on what I wanted to, I would spend exhausting energy trying not to stare or be distracted. The same neurotic symptom would include anything antisocial, impolite, or forbidden to stare at such as a person's private area.

I think that most people have heard the advice that to overcome a fear you first have to face it. I know there are modern medications and techniques to deal with all types of mental illnesses, but I tend to be a "do for yourself" type of individual. I know firsthand, during my lifetime struggle with neurosis, that the "face it" method has really helped me. I've used positive thinking quotes as mental tools. That is what has given me the necessary faith and courage to prevail.

I would try to think up a suitable positive thinking quote and repeat it over and over to myself for at least fifty or more times each day. Several years ago my imagination wanted to create nighttime monsters, so to deal with the problem I simply made up a positive thinking quote.

The quote I made up was, "I can face all threats and imaginations," then I would repeat it as many times as necessary. Thereafter I no longer had a fear of any unreasonable imagination. To deal with my neurosis of trying to concentrate and avoid overpowering distractions, I finally came up with a suitable positive thinking quote.

The positive thinking quote that I came up with is, "I can face and forgive all of my looks and actions," Then I would repeat it fifty or more times a day.
Now, to change the subject, the old folks used to say, "always remember to count your blessings." Over the years I have found that to be helpful, especially when

I'm feeling down. Things like joy and happiness in most cases is really a state of mind.

I have found that if one counts his blessings and treats all people well or like he would like to be treated even if not treated well in return, then joy and happiness won't completely desert you. The saying "that one is just about as happy as he makes up his mind to be," is true. It is not what one has or doesn't have that determines one's overall joy and happiness, but how well one appreciates what he does have.

Here are two count your blessings positive thinking quotes that I often repeat to myself: "Thank you God for my life, health, and strength, or thank you God for the way I am."

The hardest part of all for us that are suffering from neurosis and phobias is to get friends and loved ones to understand. Most confident people can't understand why anyone would fear disapproval or be affected by the seemingly little things that bother a neurotic individual.

For a neurotic individual it may take a lot of energy just to get up for even a simple occasion. Most friends and loved ones pretend to understand, but deep down many blame the victim as being somewhat selfish and unfriendly. Neurotic behavior is like many things in life. It has to be experienced firsthand to be truly understood. " So many toils and snares I have overcome " (paraphrased).

Nobody has to tell me how it feels to be laughed at, ridiculed, shamed, and humiliated. I've experienced it all firsthand. That is why I know that one who refuses to hate others and turn bitter can never be a failure or mentally destroyed. Lastly, even a minor change in behavior might bring on some stress. So, just to be

86

on the safe side myself, I take a stress vitamin daily
and see my doctor regularly.

Remember that anything mentally or physically that
doesn't destroy you will make you stronger in some
way. Facing and overcoming obstacles in life is what
makes Successful people the way they are. In my
view every super achiever was in someway searching
for love and approval, and the greatness resulted as a
by-product.

When I was a small kid I was called a cry baby
because I would cry at the drop of a hat. Well, It's
still true, it's just that I've become an expert at hiding
it. Anytime I watch a movie or read a book where a
character doesn't quit and come out on top, there are
going to be tears in my eyes. These are a few of the
personal things that

I've decided to share for the first time. Long ago I
decided not to keep a dairy because of prying eyes.
When I look back over my, life there is a lot I don't
understand, but a determination to survive always
stands out. I never set out to be a writer, but my
instinct to survive forced me to start writing for
reasons I never plan to publicly express.

I believe the Lord works in mysterious ways, and in
my case I have come to believe that I was chosen to
get the warning out. In almost every way I can think
of, writing has been bad for me. It has left me broke
and deeply in debt, and surely turned some powerful
people against me, yet there is a force within that
drives me on.

There is hardly anyone seemingly more unsuitable for
the mission than I am. My neurotic symptoms cause
me to be tense and ill at ease around people, and
before crowds it requires a lot of energy not to look
sad and pitiful. Looking back I can only surmise that

being punished regularly and harshly for wetting the bed as a small child brought on the early neurotic symptom of looking pitiful.

This kind of talk may be self-serving, but I felt a need to make a point to those that give up, or quit. All of my life I have battled shyness, low self esteem, feelings of unworthiness, lack of confidence, neurotic symptoms, self hate, etc., but quitting was not an option, wallowing in self pity was not an option, and I've never turned bitter and never will. I think of the following adages: "One monkey don't stop the show," "You can't stop the world and get off," and "Life will go on with or without you."

I learned early that hate and bitterness are destroyers, and number one on the list is the man in the mirror. I could go on and on, on how I feel like a fish out of water being a writer, but to me quitting is not an option. Amen.

"THE COUNT DOWN HAS BEGUN, CAN WE SURVIVE," it is not any kind of prediction, I just grabbed it out of thin air because I thought it would get attention. Yet, I hope the future proves it to be an untrue statement.

SPECIAL THANKS
It is said one is the result of one's whole life's experience. I would like to thank all of those that have touched my life through the years.

FREDDIE L. SIRMANS, SR.
Self Made
Writer/Publisher/Philosopher/Inventor

THE END

WEBSITE: FLSirmans.com

Race And Economic Problem Final Solution In USA

Read excerpts or buy his books on website